C210489785

CW00496460

28

5

MARY TYLER
MOORE of
the DICK VAN
DYKE SHOW

Retro TV

IAN COLLIS

NEW
HOLLAND

Introduction

What did we do before the age of television? For children of the Baby Boom age, life changed almost overnight with the introduction of TV.

Retro TV is a celebration of the formative years of the 'new medium.' In the 25-year period from the start of 1950s through to the mid-1970s, television evolved from the radio era to the modern shows we enjoy today. We look at the popular (and not so popular) shows that came and went, some all too briefly; the various stars, and the different genres of shows that invaded our homes…mostly in glorious black and white.

Before television the radiogram was a large piece of furniture, complete with space underneath for all your records and was the central focus of family entertainment. Families would gather around it at night and be entertained. In the 1950s, a new and very expensive television became the centre of entertainment in most Western countries around the world.

Children of that era were brought up on a diet of television that was almost totally dominated by American shows…and how we lapped it up. The Westerns, the variety shows and sitcoms dominated the small screen. The stars of those became heroes who would be imitated in our games in our backyards.

Television came to American households in 1948, while England had been the pioneer with broadcasting beginning in 1936 as a public service. The price of a television set in America was initially a minimum of $300. If you could afford a TV, you would have become the most popular house in the street, with neighbours, friends and relatives devising reasons to come over for a visit. People would crowd in front of a shop display window in electrical stores to watch shows. Before our family had television (1960 in our case), we would stand at the bathroom window looking at next door's television through their opened side door for a glimpse of the 'action.'

Television's first managers had backgrounds in radio, working for a network, station or advertising agency. By the 1930s, radio had become America's most popular medium, with the population spending more time listening to radio programmes than reading newspapers or viewing motion pictures. Radio time sold to advertisers totalled some $215 million in 1940, increasing to $506 million in 1947.

TV initially mimicked radio, and just as radio had filled its schedule with daily shows and weekly serials with regular casts who became familiar to listeners, television's earliest programming followed the same pattern. Programmes were transferred to the small screen…news programmes, quiz shows, dramas and comedies…with many radio performers also moving to TV.

Opposite: Jackie Gleason and Audrey Meadows as
Ralph and Alice Kramden in *The Honeymooners*.

Individual sponsors not only produced programmes but often demanded specific time slots on the evening schedule. NBC and CBS developed strategies intended to reverse this relationship. Advertisers ultimately proved willing to give up their control over programmes if the networks could guarantee large audiences. Until then, sponsors played arbitrators, in effect using their immense patronage to decide which programming strategy would prevail.

Television's early attempt to present the news struggled in the 1950s. The decade's TV journalism certainly had its moments...and its role model. Edward R. Murrow of CBS inspired a generation of TV journalists, including Ted Koppel of ABC and Bernard Shaw of CNN. Yet audiences were generally slight and advertisers unreliable. Murrow would eventually lose his place on the TV schedule and quit broadcasting altogether in 1961.

The two dominant television networks in the 1950s, CBS and NBC, had also been the nation's major radio chains. Television's first generation of executives and producers understood radio's basic commandment: the moral sensitivities of any significant portion of the great audience must not be upset. Indeed, a minority adept at letter-writing wielded extraordinary power.

If anything, the years immediately after World War II saw a renewed dedication to traditional moral values. 'On matters pertaining to sex,' wrote a network censor, 'America as a whole proclaims itself to be one way and acts another.' With returning soldiers marrying and a baby boom under way, Americans proved even more homebound in the 1950s. And, in a short period, television, like radio, became a house guest. 'Television has to be careful,' the producer Bill Todman remarked in 1953, 'because of the peculiar psychological business of going into the living room.' Remarked the actor and producer Desi Arnaz, 'You are coming into their house.'

TV, remarked one industry observer, 'must attain new heights of innocence.'

The motion picture industry had survived the spread of radio in the 1920s and 1930s and could be expected to prosper in the new television age. However, such rosy scenarios proved incorrect, with the 'Big Five' movie studios (MGM, Warner Brothers, Paramount, Columbia and Universal) waiting until the mid-1950s before entering into negotiations with the networks. By this time, they had already lost the leverage they might have enjoyed a decade earlier.

In contrast, newspaper publishers applauded television's coming. Decades earlier, daily papers had been among the earliest to operate radio stations in their communities. Investing in television, an editor and publisher reporter explained, 'affords an opportunity to carry out the principal function of a newspaper, public service. The community expects its newspaper to take the lead in furnishing it with this colourful medium of news and entertainment.'

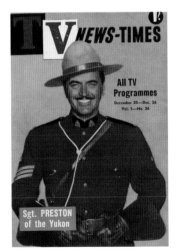

As the '50s rolled on, what was produced in that decade probably does not compare too well these days. There were initial funding restraints and moral convictions ruled much that went to air, but the possibilities were still endless, with a great sense of enthusiasm where this new medium could possibly be taken. The writing was often brilliant, unlike the formulaic shows that followed, and the performances mercurial, with many lost in the mists of time. As technical obstacles were overcome, entrepreneurs quickly followed as businessmen saw the commercial possibilities, sniffed the value of patents and dreamed of the manufacturing bonanzas. So, while in England and Europe, state-subsidised television assured its measured growth and support, in America a different model quickly evolved, with more money and more stars catapulting television as the dominant form of entertainment in our homes.

Left: This half-hour adventure series starred Richard Simmons as Sergeant Preston of the Royal Canadian Mounted Police, and ran from 1955 to 1958. *Sergeant Preston of the Yukon* on the cover of *TV News-Times* on 20 December 1958.

America had a system ready made for television: talent, both in front and behind the camera, the money from a booming, post-war economy, the studios and most importantly, the customers. Americans led the way, with a cavalcade of stars and shows having us glued to our magnificent new television sets, in glorious black and white.

Milton Berle was without doubt one of the early big stars of American television as host of *The Texaco Star Theatre Vaudeville Show*. Left to his own devices, the comic constructed the programme as a video version of his night club show and vaudeville. Firing off many jokes in a short space of time, whether directed at himself or some poor soul in the front row, conveyed the lack of subtlety in Berle's comedy but the public loved it. By the fall of 1948, Berle had become a sensation. NBC even delayed its election night coverage one hour to air the Texaco programme. 'His rating was so big,' commented one NBC executive, that 'people who did not watch Milton Berle was statistically insignificant.'

Two weeks after Berle debuted another institution was born. Ed Sullivan hosted *The Toast of the Town*. If Berle was vaudeville and burlesque, Sullivan revived legitimate variety. With his awkward mannerisms, strange posture and stiff demeanour Sullivan, a former sports reporter and Broadway columnist, would introduce the various acts, which included everything from corny dog routines to world-class ballet.

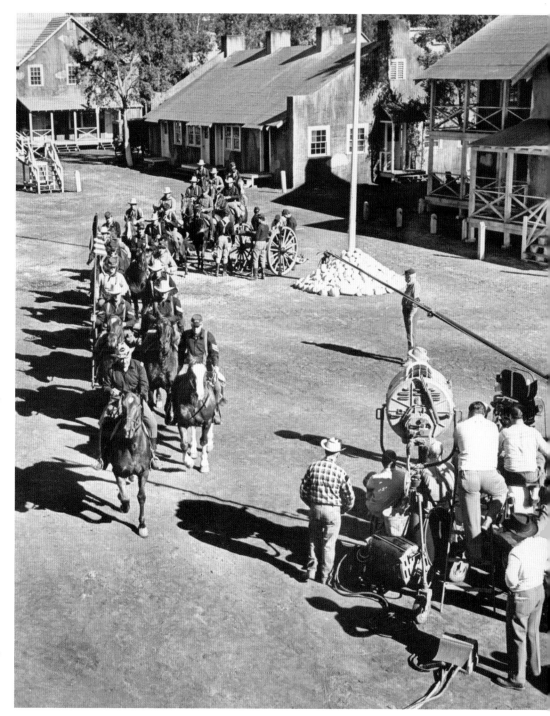

Right: A wonderful production shot of the TV series *Gunslinger* in 1961. American TV had the established infrastructure of the existing movie studios to maintain high production values on various television shows.

Later that same year, CBS introduced a live drama show that would become a pathfinder, *Studio One*. The premiere production, *The Storm*, starred actors Dean Jagger and John Forsythe, who would go on to have strong careers in television. Before the year was finished, Arthur Godfrey also debuted, simultaneously broadcasting on TV and radio *Talent Scouts*, and was a smash hit. The red-haired, freckle-faced Godfrey was very popular with his individual relaxed style, while also proving somewhat of a surprise with many of his live antics. Labelled 'vulgar' by *Time* magazine, Godfrey famously humiliated popular performer Julius LaRosa by firing him live on air. On another occasion he leered into the camera to have a 'shot' at CBS owner William Paley.

On the western front, there were none bigger than a so-called 'washed-up Hollywood actor' William Boyd, who made the transition to the small screen as *Hopalong Cassidy*. Clayton Moore was *The Lone Ranger* with his faithful Indian side-kick Tonto played by Jay Silverheels. Two of the genres 'big guns' started in the late 1950s: *Gunsmoke*, staring James Arness, and *Bonanza*, with Lorne Green as the patriarch of the Cartwright family. Both shows became television institutions, and were still on air as the 1970s rolled around. Throw in *Rin Tin Tin, Lawman, Broken Arrow, Cheyanne, Maverick, The Rifleman, Laramie, The Virginian* and *The Big Valley*, American television became synonymous with the Western 'horse opera' and sold this brand of popular culture to the rest of the world.

Another television trailblazer was comedienne Lucille Ball. With her professional life at a crossroads after a stalled movie career Ball, with husband Desi Arnaz, devised the sitcom *I Love Lucy*, which debuted in 1951. The show transformed the comedy genre—filmed live before a studio audience using a multi-camera approach—*I Love Lucy* was a sensation and Ball, a national icon. The funny redhead survived her 1960 divorce from Arnaz to reinvent the show as *The Lucy Show* and *Here's Lucy*. Desilu, the production company the pair founded, was later responsible for such classic shows as *The Untouchables, The Real McCoys, The Andy Griffith Show, My Three Sons, The Dick Van Dyke Show, Star Trek, Hogan's Heroes, Family Affair* and *Mission Impossible*.

Television was made for comedy. On 25 February 1950 *Your Show of Shows* debuted with Sid Caesar, Imogene Coca and Carl Reiner, and launched the careers of a whole generation of great comedy writers. Those who followed after, such as Ernie Kovacs, Dick Van Dyke and Rowan and Martin's *Laugh In*, owed a lot to Caesar. Others, such as film stars Jack Benny, Abbott and Costello, and Dean Martin and Jerry Lewis, found success in the medium. Movie talent of the calibre of Alfred Hitchcock, Frank Sinatra, Eddie Albert, Buddy Ebsen, Ernest Borgnine, Andy Griffiths, Fred McMurray, Gene Kelly, Robert Taylor, Shirley Booth, Donna Reed and Shirley Jones also found a home on TV in various genres. TV also launched the movie careers of Steve McQueen, James Garner, Charles Bronson, Chuck Connors, Roger Moore and Clint Eastwood, among many others.

Other names dominate these pages, of course...Jackie Gleeson, Walt Disney, Johnny Carson, Andy Williams and Carol Burnett to name a few. This book also features a diverse variety of shows and genres: family (*Ozzie and Harriet*);

Right: Dick Van Dyke was a television favourite with his award-winning *Dick Van Dyke Show* in the early 1960s. The popular comedian had mixed results when he tried to forge a film career (*Mary Poppins*, 1964 and *Chitty Chitty Bang Bang*, 1968) before finding success on TV with *Diagnosis Murder* in the 1980s.

comedy (*I Dream of Jeannie*); drama (*Dr Kildare*), war dramas (*Combat*), detective (*Burke's Law*), soap opera (*General Hospital*) and espionage shows (*The Man from UNCLE*) across three decades. After the mid 1970s, many of the programmes that followed became predictable, derivative and formulaic. Maybe we were just getting a little older and had seen it all before… only better!

I trust this book brings back many fond memories of television shows from the 'golden years' of the medium, and goes some small way to introducing these great programmes to a new generation of TV fans.

Ian Collis, June 2014

John Russell (*left*) as Marshall Dan Troop and Peter Brown as Johnny McKay in the Warner Bros. series, *Lawman* which aired from 1958–62.

Contents

Opposite: *Car 54 Where Are You?* pair
Fred Gwynne as Officer Francis Muldoon
and Joe E. Ross as Officer Gunther Toody.

The Fifties were a watershed decade for television entertainment. At the start of the decade, we depended on radio for all the news, to hear the popular songs of the day and the many serials we loved to listen to. But a few short years later television had invaded the inner sanctum of our homes and changed our lives forever. TV shows and personalities became instant stars...we laughed at Milton Berle and Lucille Ball, and the antics of *Candid Camera*; we imitated the heroes from Westerns such as *The Cisco Kid* and *Hopalong Cassidy*. We wanted a dog like *Rin Tin Tin* or *Lassie*, or to become a Mouseketeer. We wanted to fly like Superman or be the hero Zorro was. We cheered for the underdog in *The Adventures of Robin Hood*, and couldn't get enough of singers such as Frank Sinatra and Patti Page. We learnt about world events from the Walters, Cronkite and Winchell; watched game shows *What's My Line* and *You Bet Your Life*, and looked up to All-American families like *Father Knows Best* and *Ozzie and Harriet*. We were thrilled by Walt Disney's adventures and mesmerised by Alfred Hitchcock's stories. What fun we had!

Opposite: The stars of *I Love Lucy*, from left to right: Lucille Ball, Vivian Vance, Desi Arnaz and William Frawley.

1950s

I Love Lucy
(15 October 1951–24 June 1957) **CBS**

The Lucy-Desi Comedy Hour
(6 November 1957–1 April 1960) **CBS**

The half-hour *I Love Lucy* was a show of many firsts: the first sitcom to be filmed before a live audience and television's first smash-hit comedy. It ranked first for four years, second once and third in its six-year run. The stars of the show, husband and wife team Lucille Ball and Desi Arnaz, owned the show through their production company, Desilu. *I Love Lucy* was a brilliant comedy about a bandleader and his accident-prone wife—Ricky and Lucy Ricardo—who lived in a small apartment on East 68th Street, and their adventures with their frumpy neighbours, Fred and Ethel Mertz, played by William Frawley and Vivian Vance.

After *I Love Lucy* ran its course, 13 hour-long shows were filmed, known as *The Lucy-Desi Comedy Hour* and *The Lucille Ball-Desi Arnaz Show*. The last of these, 'Lucy Meets the Moustache', featured Ernie Kovacs and Edie Adams, and was especially poignant, as it was filmed after Lucy and Desi had agreed to a divorce.

Far Left: *I Love Lucy* debuted on 15 October 1951 with Lucille Ball and Desi Arnaz. In this un-aired pilot, Ricky tries to keep Lucy away from auditioning for a TV show, but when a clown becomes unavailable, Lucy steps in to take his place.

Near Left: Lucy on the cover of *TV Guide* in 1954.

14

Above: Desi Arnaz and Lucille Ball in one of their early *I Love Lucy* 'Christmas Specials'.

Right: Lucy, pictured in yet another madcap episode, had audiences in raptures with her zany antics in shows spanning three decades.

The Cisco Kid
(1950) Syndicated

After beginning on radio in 1943, the television version starred Duncan Renaldo as Cisco and Leo Carrillo as his jovial sidekick, Pancho. While in the eyes of the law, Cisco and Pancho were desperadoes, in the eyes of the poor and downtrodden, they were saviours.

Above: *The Cisco Kid* (Duncan Renaldo) and Pancho (Leo Carrillo) with beautiful guest star Jane Adams in the episode, 'The Girl from San Lorenzo'. In this episode our heroes set out to clear their names after bandits had impersonated them in a staged hold-up.

Right: *The Cisco Kid*, hero to many a young person in the 1950s. This was the first television series to be shot in colour.

get set for
HIGH ADVENTURE
every Monday at 7 pm
with "THE **CISCO KID**"
and Pancho

Channel **4** WNBT

George Reeves was cautious in his interaction with the young children who were fans of *Adventures of Superman*, as they often tried to test his 'invulnerability' by assaulting him. At one appearance a young boy came up to Reeves, pulled out a pistol and pointed it at him. The boy had taken the weapon, a Luger that his father had brought home from WWII, to see if Superman really was invulnerable. Reeves convinced the boy to give him the gun by saying that someone else would get hurt when the bullets bounced off of Superman.

Below Left: Superman adorns the cover of *TV Guide* on 25 September 1953. George Reeves found himself typecast in the role, which made it difficult for him to find work after the series ended in 1958.

Below right: Superman shows his remarkable strength by lifting *Daily Planet* reporter Lois Lane.

Adventures of Superman
(1951–1958) Syndicated

Above: 'The man of steel' shows his remarkable strength by lifting a car to demonstrate his super powers. The production budget for the Adventures of Superman was very small. To cut expenses, they would shoot all of the scenes on a particular set at one time for many different episodes. The cast weren't given enough time to change into different clothing, so you'll see the characters in the same clothes in many episodes. The cast were paid a paltry $200 per episode.

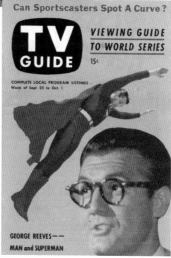

You Bet Your Life

(5 October 1950–21 September 1961) **NBC**

Television's funniest game show was emceed by 'The One, the Only' Groucho Marx. The game was almost irrelevant as Groucho interviewed each contestant. Many of the guests were non-professionals, but there were also some well-known celebrity contestants like Gary Cooper, Candice Bergen who appeared with her father Edgar Bergen, Richard Rogers and Oscar Hammerstein, Phyllis Diller and Joe Louis. At the start of each show the audience was shown a secret word, which, if any of the contestants happened to utter, a stuffed duck or a beautiful girl on a swing might drop from the ceiling with $100 attached. George Fenneman did the announcing,

Did you know?

Struggling author William Peter Blatty won $10,000 on this show. When Groucho Marx asked what he planned to do with the money, he said he planned to take some time off to 'work on a novel'. The result was *The Exorcist* (1973).

Above: John Guedel, the producer of *You Bet Your Life*, presents Groucho Marx with a tin cup commemorating the show's 12th season, which Groucho uses to ash his cigar. With Groucho's career with the Marx Brothers seemingly at an end in 1950, he impressed Guedel with his ad-libbing talent during an appearance with Bob Hope. Guedel subsequently signed Groucho for the hosting role, which proved a master-stroke.

Far left: Groucho's expert announcer George Fenneman and the adorable Ginny Tiu who appeared on *You Bet Your Life* in the late 1950s. Fenneman was also the target for the rapier-like wit and sarcastic asides of Groucho.

Near left: Groucho and his lovely production assistant Marianne Gaba on 'The Best of Groucho' in 1955.

Love That Bob
(The Bob Cummings Show)

(2 January 1955–25 September 1955) **NBC**
(1 September 1955–19 September 1957) **CBS**
(24 September 1957–15 September 1959) **NBC**

Left: *Love That Bob* starred Robert Cummings (*centre*) as Bob Collins, a girl-crazy photographer. Ann B. Davis (*left*) played Schultzy, his secretary, Rosemary DeCamp, as Margaret MacDonald (*right*), Bob's widowed sister, Dwayne Hickman as Chuck MacDonald her son and Joi Lansing as Shirley Swanson, the buxom model who chased after Bob.

Below: Inge Goude, former Miss Sweden, takes a dim view of Dwayne Hickman's analysis of Bob Cummings who plays his uncle in *Love That Bob*.

19

The George Burns and Gracie Allen Show
(12 October 1950–22 September 1958) **CBS**

George Burns and Gracie Allen had one of the most enduring acts in the history of show-business.
The show format was simple enough; set in the Burns home, George played himself in the dual role of on-screen narrator and straight man for Gracie's scatterbrained antics. Burns would simply turn to the camera, cigar in hand, and philosophise to the audience.

Right: George and Gracie on the cover of *TV Guide* on 8 October 1955. Gracie Allen died in 1964, but Burns went on to have a long career on TV and in movies, stretching to his 100th year in 1996.

TV GUIDE
COWBOY ALBUM

The Gene Autry Show
(23 July 1950–7 August 1956) **CBS**

For six seasons Gene Autry (*left*) and his sidekick, Pat Buttram (later of *Green Acres* fame), rode from town to town helping maintain law and order. Each episode provided opportunities for Gene to sing, Pat to get into trouble, and Autry's horse 'Champion' to show off some trick or other.

Hopalong Cassidy
(24 June 1949–23 December 1951) **NBC**
(1952–1954) **Syndicated**

Below: William Boyd first starred as Hopalong Cassidy, a western hero who dressed in black and rode a white horse, in 66 movie features filmed between 1935 and 1948. The TV plots were the same as the old films, with a silver-haired Hoppy chasing villains to their doom on his faithful horse, Topper.

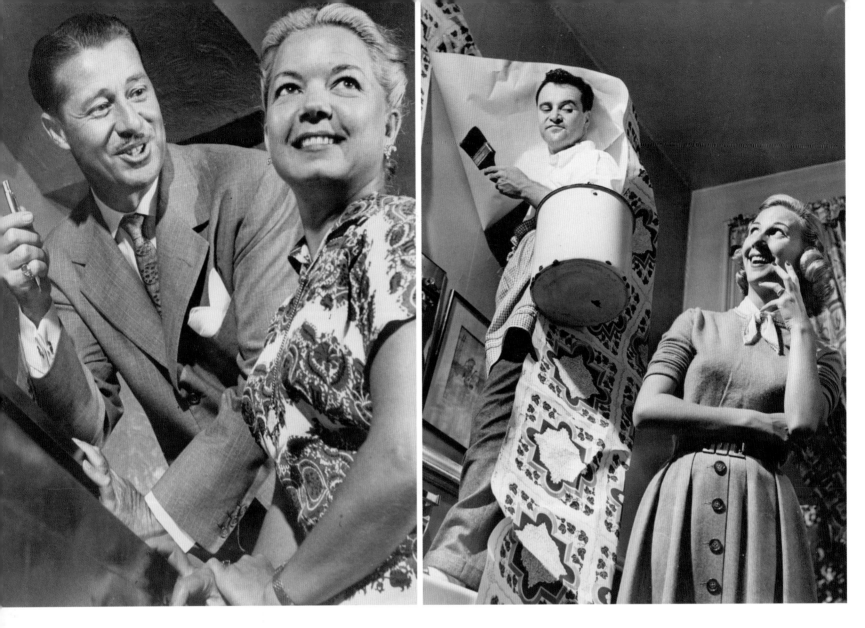

The Frances Langford-Don Ameche Show

(10 September 1951–14 March 1952) **ABC**

Frances Langford and Don Ameche hosted this daytime variety hour. A singer and entertainer, Langford was very popular during the golden age of radio, performing with Bob Hope on his *Pepsodent Show* from 1941 while also appearing in films from the mid-1930s to the early 1950s. Ameche was already an established movie star (*The Story of Alexander Graham Bell*, 1939), but made a comeback in the 1980s when well into his 70s and won an Oscar for Best Supporting Actor in *Cacoon* (1985).

Above right: A regular feature of the show was 'The Couple Next Door', with Jack Lemmon and Cynthia Stone playing a young married couple.

Blind Date

(5 May 1949–20 September 1951) **ABC**
(7 June 1952–19 July 1952) **NBC**
(9 June 1953–15 September 1953) **Dumont**

Blind Date began on radio in 1943. It was the first TV game show to be hosted by a woman.

Right: The very charming Arlene Francis as hostess of *Blind Date*, with announcer Rex Marshall.

Beat the Clock

(23 March 1950–12 September 1958) **CBS**
(13 October 1958–30 January 1961) **ABC**
(1960–1974) **Syndicated**
(17 September 1979–1 February 1980) **CBS**

Below: On *Beat the Clock*, couples were required to perform various stunts within a certain time period (usually less than one minute). The winning couple was given the chance to try a special stunt for a larger prize. The stunt was quite difficult and would be attempted weekly until someone was able to perform it. Bud Collyer, who hosted, is having a great time watching the contestant trying to name the flavour of each ice cream in the required time.

Did you know?

In 1952, a young unemployed actor got his first job in TV testing stunts and warming-up audiences on *Beat the Clock*. His name was James Dean.

23

Arthur Godfrey and His Friends

(12 January 1949–28 April 1959) **CBS**

Arthur Godfrey and His Friends was an hour-long variety show. He was also arguably one of television's earliest commercial pitchmen, also known by the nickname 'Old Redhead'. The show itself was a variety hour built around Godfrey and his friends, but he would frequently throw away his script and improvise his way through a commercial. Controversial, Godfrey enjoyed a love hate relationship with the media, but he enjoyed enormous clout with the new medium in the 1950s.

Did you know?

Arthur Godfrey fired singer Julius LaRosa at the end of a show in 1953 while it was still being broadcast on radio after the television broadcast had ended. Godfrey's popularity went downhill after that.

Art Linkletter on the cover of *TV Guide* on 6 August 1955.

Art Linkletter

(6 October 1950–25 April 1952) **ABC**
(18 February 1963–16 September 1963 **NBC**
(29 December 1969–25 September 1970) **NBC**

Art Linkletter's House Party

(1 September 1952–5 September 1969)

Art Linkletter's opening foray into television with *Life with Linkletter* was a version of the previous *Art Linkletter's House Party*, which had begun on radio. Both shows featured audience-participation stunts to win prizes and interviews with schoolchildren. Their unrehearsed remarks were fodder for a series of best-selling books by Linkletter, the first of which was *Kids Say the Darndest Things*. After *House Party* finished, Linkletter returned with his son to co-host on NBC a daytime remake of *Life with Linkletter*.

Annie Oakley
(1952–1956) **Syndicated**

Gail Davis (left) who starred as Annie Oakley from 1954–1956, made her motion picture debut in 1947 before landing a supporting role under Roy Rogers in a western the following year. By 1950, she began to secure guest roles in television westerns, appearing in *The Cisco Kid* on numerous occasions. Set in the town of Diablo, Gail Davis played Annie Oakley, a gun-toting rancher. Gail Davis was an excellent rider and trick-shooter in real life. She actually performed in Gene Autry's travelling rodeo show.

Below: Annie Oakley on the cover of *TV News-Times* on 17 January 1959.

Candid Camera

(10 August 1948–3 December 1948) **ABC**
(29 May 1949–18 August 1949) **NBC**
(12 September 1949–25 September 1950) **CBS**
(27 August 1951–23 May 1952) **ABC**
(2 June 1953–5 August 1953) **NBC**
(2 October 1960–3 September 1967) **CBS**
(1974–1978) **Syndicated**

Allen Funt (*left*) created and hosted this hilarious show in which people were filmed with a hidden camera. Many of the situations were staged, but other situations were not contrived and featured the best and worst of human nature. Funt assumed disguises weekly, surprising unsuspecting citizens in unusual circumstances with the catchphrase, 'Smile, you're on candid camera!' CBS aired some specials during the 1989–90 season, with Funt's son, Peter, joining his dad as co-host.

The Ken Murray Show
(15 April 1950–7 June 1952, 8 February 1953–14 June 1953) **CBS**

Vaudevillian Ken Murray hosted an hour-long variety show on Saturday nights for two seasons. His show featured top-name guest stars of the day with elaborate sets as a backdrop, including his trademark Hollywood and Vine backdrop. Ken bridged the various acts with informal chatter and humour.

Did you know?

Over the course of his career, Murray filmed many Hollywood celebrities (including Douglas Fairbanks, Mary Pickford, Charlie Chaplin and Jean Harlow) using his 16mm home movie camera, sending back the footage to his grandparents instead of writing letters. The footage would years later used in several television specials about Hollywood.

Left: Ken Murray and the 'Glamourlovelies' on *The Ken Murray Show* in late December 1951.

Below: Kirk Douglas (*left*) re-enacted two dramatic scenes from *Champion*, the movie that sky-rocketed him to overnight stardom in 1949 on *The Ken Murray Show* in February 1950.

28

Milton Berle–The Milton Berle Show (The Texaco Star Theatre)

(21 September 1948–9 June 1953) **NBC**

The Milton Berle Show

(27 September 1955–5 June 1956) **NBC**

The Milton Berle Show

(9 September 1966–6 January 1967) **ABC**

The most popular hour of the week during the early years of television was watching Milton Berle, on every Tuesday evening. It was reported that Milton Berle 'Mr Television' sold more TV sets than any advertising campaign. People wanted to watch him...his sight gags, outlandish costumes and props. Berle remained a popular performer on television long after his regular show finished in 1956.

Right: Three of the very best of the entertainment industry of their day, (*from left to right*) Milton Berle, Bing Crosby and Jimmy Durante in the 1960s.

Below: Milton Berle has his hands full with a line of gorgeous bathing beauties in October 1954.

The Roy Rogers Show

(30 December, 1951–9 June 1957) **NBC**

Left: Roy Rogers and Dale Evans appeared in both film and televisions episodes together, along with his golden palomino horse, Trigger, and his German Shepherd dog, Bullet. The shows usually featured sidekick George 'Gabby' Hayes, Pat Brady or Andy Devine. Rogers was an idol for many children of the day. Rogers and Evans' famous theme song, *Happy Trails*, which they sang together to sign off their television show, was written by Evans.

Below: Roy Rogers, cowboy star on the cover of *TV News-Times* on 4 July 1959.

Scotland Yard

(1953–1961) UK

Filmed in England, this series presented dramas based on actual cases from the files of Scotland Yard. Series host Edgar Lustgarten was a noted English criminologist. An action-drama series with stories taken from the files of London's renowned detective bureau, it showed the Yard's men in action against the authentic backgrounds of cities throughout Europe, Asia and Africa.

The Line-up/San Francisco Beat

(1 October 1954–20 January 1960) CBS

Produced in cooperation with the San Francisco Police Department, *The Line-up* gave realistic, semi-documentary portrayals of the work of law officers. Det. Lt. Ben Guthrie, played by Warner Anderson (*below*), and Inspector Matt Grebb, played by Tom Tully, were the officers who tracked down criminals. The stories were all based on actual cases and generally included a police line-up where the victims of the crime attempted to pick out the perpetrators.

FRIDAYS 9.30

You'll thrill to the powerful and compelling drama of "San Francisco Beat" every Friday night at 9.30 as the law fights an unending battle to maintain peace and order in modern-day San Francisco.

Stay in line with

CHANNEL 9

The Grind That Godfrey Couldn't Take

—See Page 10

PENN-NY
TV
GUIDE

LOCAL PROGRAM LISTINGS
WEEK OF MAY 12—18

15c

The Adventures of Robin Hood
(1955–1959)

Filmed on location in England, this popular UK series brought the famous swashbuckler to American television. Donald Pleasence (later *The Great Escape*, 1963) was Prince John and the Sheriff of Nottingham was played by Alan Wheatley. The series starred Richard Greene (*right*) with Maid Marian played by Bernadette O'Farrell (*left*) and later Patricia Driscoll. Other cast included Alexander Gauge as Friar Tuck and Ian Hunter as Richard the Lionheart. Paul Eddington played more than 20 different parts before being given the regular role of Will Scarlet, one of the merry men.

Did you know?

The stirring title song (*Robin Hood, Robin Hood, riding through the glen!*) was sung by Dick James, later the music publisher of The Beatles.

Left: Bernadette O'Farrell and Richard Greene on the cover of *TV Guide* on 12 May 1956.

Below: Robin Hood defends Maid Marian from the Sheriff of Nottingham's soldiers.

32

The Lone Ranger

(15 September 1949–12 September 1957) **ABC**

Each episode of the *The Lone Ranger* opened with Moore riding 'Silver', a magnificent white stallion, galloping along to the strains of *The William Tell Overture*. Silver would then rear up with the Lone Ranger shouting, 'Hi-ho, Silver!'—Stirring stuff!

Did you know?

In Spanish, the name Tonto means 'fool' or 'moron', so the name was dubbed as 'Toro' for Spanish audiences.

Left and below: Clayton Moore as The Lone Ranger, a fictional masked former Texas Ranger who fights injustice in the old west.

The Loretta Young Show
(20 September 1953–10 September 1961) **NBC**

The Loretta Young Show was a series of individual stories dealing with the nobler side of the human spirit. Oscar-winning actress Loretta Young (*The Farmer's Daughter*, 1947) would sweep through a doorway and move into the centre of the room to introduce the evening's play. She would end the show by reading a few lines of poetry or a passage from the bible that restated the message of telecast.

Below: Loretta Young with Bruce Banick and Gina Gillespie on the episode titled 'Day of Rest' aired in May, 1958.

Dagmar's Canteen

(22 March 1952–14 June 1952) **NBC**

Dagmar with announcer Robert Q. Lewis on 'The Name's the Same'. This short-lived 15-minute variety series hosted by Dagmar (Jennie Lewis) presented talent culled from the armed forces. A feature of each week's show was when the guest celebrity described whom he or she would most like to be.

Right: The very popular Dagmar on the cover of TV Guide on 18 August 1951.

The Jack Paar Show

(13 November 1953–4 September 1954, 4 July 1955–25 May 1956) **CBS**

The Jack Paar Programme

(21 September 1962–10 September 1965) **NBC**

Comedian Jack Paar (*above and right*) served as host of this live summer daytime replacement for *My Favourite Husband*. The format of *The Jack Paar Show* included monologues by Jack, appearances by guest artists and songs by his regular singers. A quick-witted master of ceremonies, he is best known for his stint as host of *The Tonight Show* from 1957 to 1962. After this he was given a Friday primetime hour show, *The Jack Paar Show*, which ran from 1962 to 1965. *The Jack Paar Programme* later moved to Friday night and followed a similar format to his previous show.

Above: Jack Paar interviews Zsa Zsa Gabor and Jayne Mansfield in 1963.

Did you know?

Paar's programme was the first American variety show to present The Beatles. Film clips of the band were shown on 3 January 1964, more than a month before the group's famous 'debut' on *The Ed Sullivan Show*.

The Jack Benny Programme

(28 October 1950–15 September 1964) **CBS**
(25 September 1964–10 September 1965) **NBC**

The ever-popular Jack Benny (*right*) entered television with a variety show featuring situation comedy, singing and dancing. After a successful radio career starting in 1932, Benny brought across many of his proven supporting players, including Eddie Anderson as Valet, Rochester Van Jones and Don Wilson as his announcer. A comedic genius with impeccable timing, he landed many top guests on his shows including Frank Sinatra, Claudette Colbert, Basil Rathbone (1951) and a very young Johnny Carson (1952), while both Marilyn Monroe and Humphrey Bogart also made their television debuts during the 1953–54 season.

Near right: Comedian Bob Hope struggles to keep in character as funny man Jack Benny does not keep to the script during a scene on the show.

Far right: Jack Benny on the cover of *TV Guide* on 5 February 1954

Tales of the Texas Rangers
(3 September 1955–25 May 1957) **CBS**

Tales of the Texas Rangers followed the exploits of one of America's most famous law-enforcement agencies. Although Ranger Jace Pearson (Willard Parker) and Ranger Clay Morgan (Harry Lauter) were regulars, they appeared in a different setting each week, ranging from the old west of the 1830s to modern-day Texas, using crime-detection methods appropriate to each era. The show had a memorable opening sequence with white-shirted rangers walking down a road, their numbers growing as the camera panned back.

Did you know?

Captain Manuel T. 'Lone Wolf' Conzaullas who was said to have killed 31 men during his 30-year career as a Texas ranger, was the consultant for the series.

Left: Harry Lauter and Willard Parker of *Tales of the Texas Rangers*.

Below: Rangers Jace Pearson (Willard Parker, *left*) and Clay Morgan (Harry Lauter) get their man with the help of shortwave radio in this episode.

The Adventures of Rin Tin Tin

(15 October 1954–28 August 1959) **ABC**

The main cast of *The Adventures of Rin Tin Tin*, (*from left to right*) James Brown as Lt. Rip Masters, Lee Aaker as Rusty, Rand Brooks as Corporal Randy Boone, Joe Sawyer as Sgt. Biff O'Hara and German Shepherd wonder-dog, Rin Tin Tin. Rusty and his dog Rin Tin Tin (played by Rinty and his offspring) had been orphaned and were adopted by the cavalry soldiers at Fort Apache, Arizona.

Above top right: Rin Tin Tin with James Brown on the cover of *Television Week* on 4 May 1957

Above bottom right: Lee Aaker played Rusty on *The Adventures of Rin Tin Tin*. Like many child actors, Aaker's career did not transfer into adulthood. He also lost the juvenile role in the classic *Shane* (1953) to Brandon DeWilde.

The Frank Sinatra Show

(7 October 1950–1 April 1952) **CBS**
(18 October 1957–27 June 1958) **ABC**

Frank Sinatra's first show on television was a 60-minute musical variety show in the 1950–1951 season, which surprisingly failed to rate during its first year and was reduced to half an hour opposite Milton Berle's top-rating show. Like all of Berle's competition, the show quickly perished. Sinatra's second attempt at a series again proved unsuccessful, despite a reported $3 million budget. The series was a combination of drama and musical programmes but the show was cancelled after just one season.

Left: Jack Benny and Frank Sinatra in 1951 with Jack discussing the script of his second television show with Frank.

Below: Film beauty and a big favourite for many, Kim Novak brought her special charm to the premiere of *The Frank Sinatra Show*, on its on 10 October 1957 airing. Also appearing this night were Bob Hope and Peggy Lee.

Above left: Ethel Merman hits a musical comedy note as she presents some of the songs she made famous on Broadway, later joining Frank to perform together in April 1958.

Above right: June Hutton's lovely voice was an attraction on *The Frank Sinatra Show*. Miss Hutton was the younger sister of the well-known female band leader of the day Ina Ray Hutton, and the wife of Sinatra's orchestra conductor, Axel Stordahl.

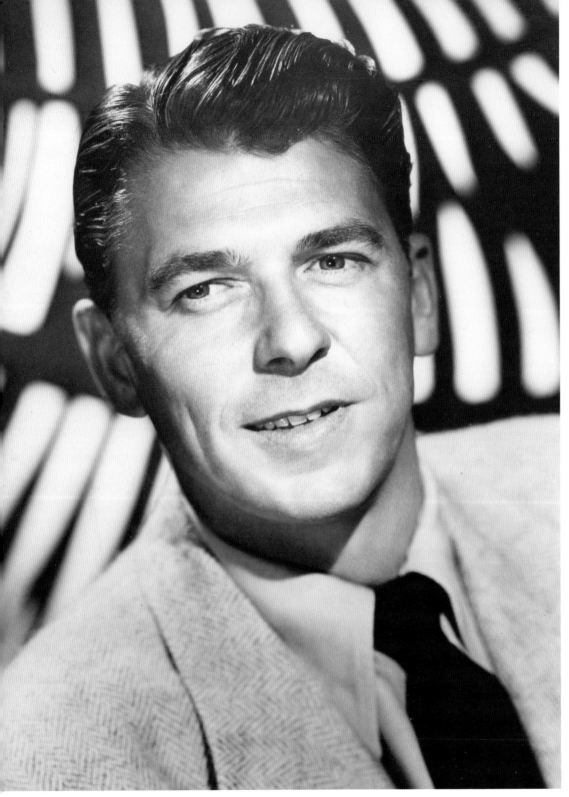

Above: Piper Laurie as Cleopatra in a 1961 episode of *General Electric Theatre.*

The General Electric Theatre
(1 February 1953–16 September 1962) CBS

Hosted by actor Ronald Reagan, this anthology drama series covered a vast emotional territory. One week's story might be an adventure and the next week a Biblical drama. It showed everything from light comedy to heavy melodrama to westerns. The list of famous performers appearing on the show included Alan Ladd, Fred MacMurray, James Stewart, Myrna Loy, Bette Davis, Tony Curtis, Fred Astaire, Sammy Davis Jr, Peggy Lee, Jane Wyman (Reagan's first wife), Myrna Loy, Jack Benny, Bette Davis and Barbara Stanwyck.

The Red Buttons Show

(14 October 1952–14 June 1954) **CBS**
(1 October 1954–27 May 1955) **NBC**

Comedian, singer and actor, Red Buttons (right) was a star on Broadway, won an Oscar for best supporting actor in *Sayonara* (1957) and also appeared in many other films (including *Winged Victory* and *The Longest Day*). In 1952 he was given his own variety television series, *The Red Buttons Show*, which in its three-year history was very successful.

He also recorded a two-sided hit record *Strange Things Are Happening* with *The Ho Ho Song*, which became something of a national craze with young children. Picked up by NBC in October 1954 when the format began to sag, it stayed as a variety show before changing to a situation comedy.

Below: Red Buttons on the cover of *TV Guide* on 16 October 1954

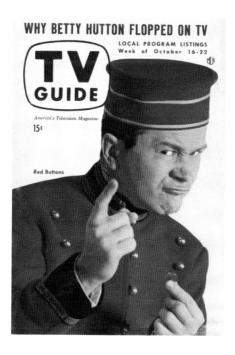

The People Who Brought Us the News

Journalist Walter Cronkite (*left*) became an American institution reporting on many events in history on television, including the Cold War, the murders of President John F. Kennedy and Martin Luther King Jr., the Vietnam protests, the Watergate break-in and the Moon Landings to name just a few. Regarded as 'the most trusted man in America', he would always sign-off with his broadcasts with the words, 'And that's the way it was'.

Below left: Famous for his on-the-spot radio reports From London during World War II, journalist Edward R. Murrow became a pioneer of television news broadcasting, producing a series of TV news reports that lead to the censure of Senator Joseph McCarthy.

Below centre: Walter Winchell, Ed Sullivan and Barry Gray on the cover of *TV Guide* on 24 October 1952.

Below right: Gossip columnist Walter Winchell was America's number-one reporter in the 1940s and early 1950s, with his own show broadcast on the ABC radio and TV networks. Feared by many because of the influence and power he wielded in show business, his syndicated newspaper column was read by 50 million people a day, while his Sunday-night radio broadcast was heard by another 20 million people up to the late 1950s. Winchell also narrated *The Untouchables* for four seasons from 1959.

Steve Donovan, Western Marshall
(September 1955–June 1956) **Syndication**

Above: Douglas Kennedy as Marshall Steve Donovan and Eddy Waller as his sidekick, Rusty Lee, are held up at gunpoint by Dave Garner in a September 1955 episode.

Right: Steve Donovan (Douglas Kennedy) protects frightened widow Laura Elliott (Belle Adams) in an episode of *Steve Donovan, Western Marshall.*

45

What's My Line

(2 February 1950–3 September 1967) **CBS**
(1968–1975) **Syndicated**

At the time, television's longest-running prime-time game show saw a panel of four celebrities trying to guess the occupations of the contestants. The panellists were permitted to ask yes-or-no questions, and the contestant was awarded $5 each time a 'no' answer was given, and if ten 'no' answers were given. The game concluded and the contestant won the top prize of $50. Each week a mystery guest would also drop by, and the panellists, who would be blindfolded, tried to guess his or her or multiple identities (in the case of couple or groups of people). John Daly, who also anchored the evening news on ABC, hosted the show for the entire 17 years on CBS. Some of the hundreds of mystery guests to appear on the show included James Cagney, Bette Davis, Walt Disney, Judy Garland, Alfred Hitchcock, Jayne Mansfield, Ronald Reagan, Edward G Robinson, Frank Sinatra, Lucille Ball, Barbara Streisand and Elizabeth Taylor.

Did you know?

Lucille Ball holds the record for the most appearances as mystery guest...five plus two with Desi.

Above: By the end of the 1950s the regular panellists of the show were (*from left to right*) Arlene Francis, Bennett Cerf, Dorothy Kilgallen, with host John Daly.

Left Steve Allen, also a popular regular of the panel, on the cover of *TV News-Times* on 13 December 1958.

Wild Bill Hickok
(1951–1956) **Syndicated**

A 30-minute western starring Guy Madison as
US Marshall James Butler (Wild Bill) Hickok,
and Andy Devine as his sidekick, Jingles B Jones
('Wait fer me, Wild Bill!'). Rugged, handsome
Guy Maddison starred in the title role of Wild Bill
Hickok, the hard-fighting US marshal who made
his name a by-word for courage in a nearly lawless
territory.

Below: No *Wild Bill Hickok* episode would be
complete without the warm, sunny disposition of Bill's
sidekick Jingles, played by Andy Devine. Devine's
inimitably gravelly voice was the result of a childhood
accident when he fell with a stick in his mouth.

Above: Sid Caesar, Imogene Coca and Carl Reiner.

Your Show of Shows
(25 February 1950–5 June 1954) **NBC**

Your Show of Shows was a one of the classics of television's 'Golden Age', and was a Saturday night fixture for millions of fans. It was 90 minutes of live, original comedy, every week…and it was brilliant! Not really a showcase for guest stars, it showcased the comedic talents of its stars Sid Caeser and Imogene Coca. Supporting them were the talented Carl Reiner and Howard Morris. The main segment of the show was a satire of a popular film, followed by the talented Caesar, a skilled mime and a superb comic actor, doing a monologue or pantomime. In addition to writers Mel Tolkin and Licille Kallen, other talents included Mel Brooks (later *Get Smart*), Larry Gelbart (*MASH*), Bill Persky and Sam Denoff (who both worked with Carl Reiner on *The Dick Van Dyke Show*), Neil Simon (*The Odd Couple*) and future film director Woody Allen. Sid Caesar brought his own unique style to the show, often deviating from the script, he was also especially when paired with Imogene Coca.

Did you know?

Your Show of Shows was the inspiration for the 1982 film, *My Favorite Year*, produced by Mel Brooks; the 2001 TV movie, *Laughter on the 23rd Floor*, written by Neil Simon; and *The Dick Van Dyke Show* television series, created by Carl Reiner.

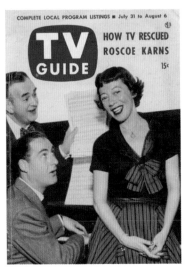

Left: Sid Caesar, Imogene Coca on the cover of *TV Guide* on 31 July 1953.

The George Gobel Show

(2 October 1954–10 March 1959) **NBC**
(11 October 1959–5 June 1960) **CBS**

The George Gobel Show starring Gobel (*right*)
pictured here with actor Joe Flynn, later of *McHale's
Navy* fame, as a pharmacist. Gobel had a quiet,
homespun style of humour, which proved popular
in the day and made him one of the biggest comedy
stars of the 1950s.

Above: The beautiful Barbara Eden
with then husband Michael Ansara
in the late 1950s.

Broken Arrow

(25 September 1956–23 September 1958) **ABC**

Starring Michael Ansara as Cochise, chief of the Apaches, and John Lupton as Indian Agent Tom Jeffords, *Broken Arrow* was one of the few westerns to show American Indians in a positive light. It adopted the novel approach of making friends with the Indians, instead of shooting them. Together, they fought both renegades from the Chiricahua Reservation and dishonest white eyes who preyed on the Indians.

Above: Tom Jeffords (John Lupton) is circled by a menacing band of Apache braves as he seeks a meeting with their chief in an episode of *Broken Arrow*.

Above: Michael Ansara (*right*), John Lupton (*left*) and the director discuss an episode in 1958.

Right: Angie Dickinson started her television career debuting on *Death Valley Days* in 1954, followed quickly by roles in *Buffalo Bill Jr.*, *It's a Great Life*, *Gray Ghost*, *Broken Arrow*, *The People's Choice*, *Gunsmoke*, *The Virginian* and *Cheyenne* to name a few. She would go on of course to have a memorable movie career, while also star as 'Pepper' Anderson in the ground-breaking series, *Police Woman* (1974).

51

Our Miss Brooks
(3 October 1952–21 September 1956) **CBS**

The Eve Arden Show
(17 September 1957–25 March 1958) **CBS**

Eve Arden starred as schoolteacher Connie Brooks and Robert Rockwell was biology teacher
Philip Boynton in the sitcom *Our Miss Brooks*.

Did you know?

Eve Arden's real name was Eunice Quedens. She decided that she needed a stage name, and she
chose it while shopping for cosmetics and spotting the names 'Evening in Paris' and 'Elizabeth Arden'.

Above: Gale Gordon, as the crusty principal Osgood Conklin, is none too pleased with Eve Arden in an episode
of *Our Miss Brooks*.

Right: Eve Arden and Gale Gordon on the cover of the 26 March 1955 issue of *TV Guide*.

52

Sea Hunt
(1957–1961) Syndicated

Right: Lloyd Bridges in his role as Mike Nelson, a former US Navy frogman, who freelanced as a scuba diver and had countless adventures rescuing people, outmanoeuvring villains and searching for lost treasure. The series proved a valuable opportunity for some of Hollywood's younger actors, namely Leonard Nimoy, Robert Conrad, Larry Hagman, Jack Nicholson and Bridge's own teenage sons, Beau and Jeff.

Below: Lloyd Bridges on the cover of *TV News-Times* on 27 June 1959. *Sea Hunt* was extremely popular in its day in part because scuba diving was very new to the public at large at that time and underwater shots of the ocean environment were very exciting to audiences. *Sea Hunt* incorporated a voice-over by Bridges, talking to the audience about what the character was thinking and planning.

The Phil Silvers Show/Sergeant Bilko

(20 September 1955–11 September 1959) **CBS**

Created and also written by Nat Hiken, the show won three consecutive Emmy Awards in the 1950s. The show's success catapulted Phil Silvers to stardom. The series was set in Fort Baxter and centred on the soldiers of the motor pool under the control of Master Sergeant Ernest G. Bilko. Bilko spent precious little time performing his duties, instead creating various get-rich-quick scams or finding ways to get others to do his work for him. The main cast included Harvey Lembeck (Cpl. Rocco Barbella), Allan Melvin (Cpl. Steve Henshaw), Paul Ford (Col. John T Hall), Herbie Faye (Pvt. Sam Fender), and Maurice Gosfield (Pvt. Duane Doberman). Sgt. Rupert Ritzik and Mrs Ritzik were played by Joe E Ross and Beatrice Pons, who were also featured as a married couple in *Car 54 Where Are You?*

Left: Private Doberman (Maurice Gosfield) gets the brush from his pals when he tries to find a date for his sister in an hilarious episode of Bilko.

Below: Sergeant Hogan (*right*) and the other WACs admire Sergeant Bilko's toupee in an 1956 episode.

Above top right: Bilko and his colonel, played by character actor Paul Ford.

Above: Sgt Bilko finds bliss with a new girlfriend, dance teacher Ellen Hodges (Hildy Parks), who is introduced on the episode, 'You'll Never Get Rich'.

Above bottom right: Phil Silvers and Elisabeth Fraser on the cover of *TV News* on 13 September 1958.

Did you know?

The original title of this series was *You'll Never Get Rich*. It was changed to *The Phil Silvers Show* less than two months after the start of the series with the original title remaining as a subtitle. Later, in syndication, the title was simplified to *Sgt Bilko*.

The Liberace Show

(1 July 1952–28 August 1952) **NBC**
(1953–1955) **Syndicated**
(13 October 1958–10 April 1959) **ABC**
(15 July 1969–16 September 1969) **CBS**

Before the sequins and hairpiece, Liberace, the flamboyant pianist with the cheesy, pearly-tooth smile, hosted a 15-minute series on Tuesdays and Thursdays during the summer of 1952. While older woman loved him, the critics savaged him. With moderate success, he then hosted a much more successful 30-minute show, which also featured his brother George as violinist and orchestra leader.

Below: Liberace on the cover of *TV Guide* in the 1950s.

The Danny Thomas Show/Make Room for Daddy

(29 September 1953–18 July 1957) **ABC**
(7 October 1957–14 September 1964) **CBS**

Make Room for Daddy, as it was known for the first three seasons before changing to *The Danny Thomas Show* was based on Thomas's own life as an entertainer and the problems created by his frequent absences from his children, Danny played nightclub entertainer Danny Williams who was constantly being upstaged by his kids—son Rusty (played by Rusty Hamer) and Terry (played by Penney Parker). Jean Hagen (*Singing in the Rain*) played Danny's wife Margaret, but Hagen quit the show in 1956 and instead of replacing her, Thomas killed her off in the show. During the 1956–1957 season Danny courted various women, before marrying Kathy, played by Marjorie Lord.

Left: A rare shot of Danny Thomas live on set.

Left: Live on set of *The Danny Thomas Show* with Jean Hagen as the serious but loving wife Margaret his wife of the first three seasons.

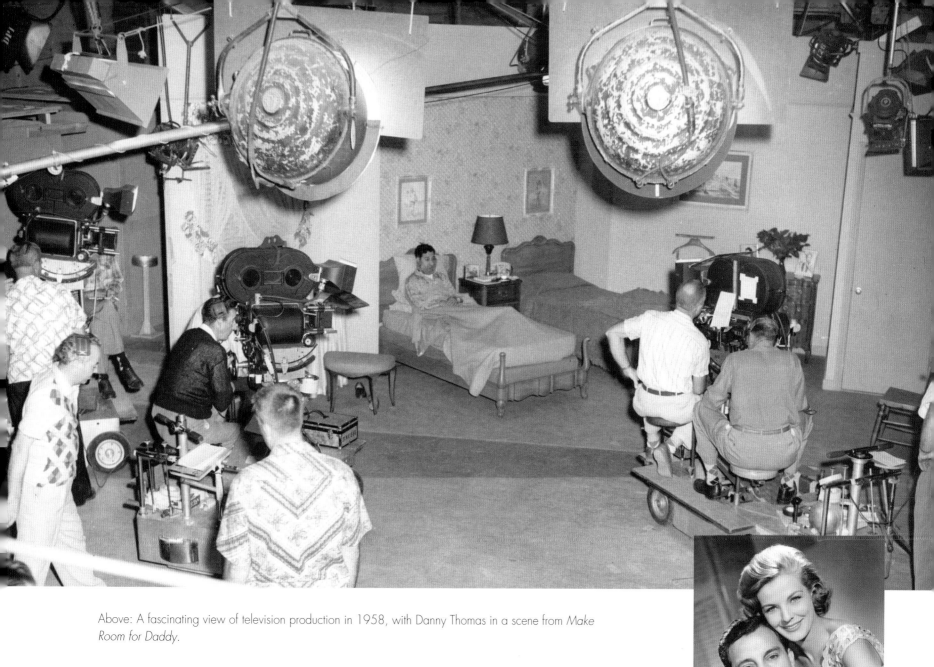

Above: A fascinating view of television production in 1958, with Danny Thomas in a scene from *Make Room for Daddy*.

Did you know?

The original title came from a phrase used in the real-life Thomas household, whenever Danny Thomas returned home from a tour, his children had to move back into their bedrooms to *Make Room for Daddy*.

Right: Danny Thomas and Marjorie Lord (who joined the show in the fourth season).

The Mickey Mouse Club

(3 October 1955–24 September 1959) **ABC**

Unlike other popular children's shows of the day, *The Mickey Mouse Club* did not use a studio audience and instead it employed a group of child performers: the T-shirted, mouse-hatted company was known as the Mouseketeers. The Mouseketeers sang, danced, starred in the filmed serials, introduced cartoons and provided an audience for the guest stars and talent acts.

Top left: The Big Mouseketeer of *The Mickey Mouse Club*, Jimmie Dodd, the original presenter and music composer and the head Mouseketeer.

Top right: Mouseketeer Darlene Gillespie on the cover of *TV News-Times* on October 16, 1959.

Bottom right: Annette Funicello (*left*) and Jymme Shaw of *The Micky Mouse Club* on the cover of *TV News-Times* on 20 June 1959.

Circus Boy

(23 September 1956–8 September 1957) **NBC**
(19 September 1957–11 September 1958) **ABC**

A children's western starring Mickey Braddock as Corky, a boy whose parents were killed in a highwire accident. Robert Lowery starred as Big Tim Champion, the owner of the circus and guardian of Corky; Noah Beery Jr. was Uncle Joey, one of the clowns, and perennial John Wayne favourite Guinn 'Big Boy' Williams was Pete, a roustabout.

Right: *Circus Boy's* Micky Braddock with one of the monkeys from the circus. Mickey's real name was George Michael Dolenz, son of character actor George Dolenz Jr, and he later achieved stardom as one of the members of 60s pop band The Monkees.

Did you know?

Mickey Dolenz was not blond as a boy; the producers made him dye his hair that colour.

Near right: Robert Lowery as Big Tim Champion.

Far right: Micky Braddock (Dolenz) as Corky with Noah Beery Jr., as Uncle Joey, one of the clowns.

Father Knows Best

(1954–1959) CBS

Left: *Father Knows Best* cast (*from left to right*) Robert Young as James 'Jim' Anderson, Elinor Donahue as Betty 'Princess' Anderson, Lauren Chapin as Kathy 'Kitten' Anderson, Billy Gray as James 'Bud' Anderson Jr. and Jane Wyatt as Margaret Anderson.

Below: The Andersons minus Mum (*from left to right*) Elinor Donahue, Robert Young, Lauren Chapin and Billy Gray on the cover of *TV Guide* on 16 June 1956. Previously on radio, only Robert Young moved to the television series.

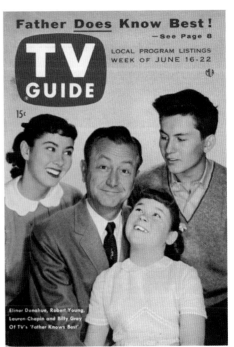

Above: Breakfast at an idealised American family home in *Father Knows Best*.

Near right: Jane Wyatt won three Emmy Awards for Best Actress in a Comedy Series as devoted wife and mother Margaret Anderson, playing opposite Robert Young winning her. In 1967, she portrayed Spock's mother in a 1967 Star Trek episode as well as in the 1986 film *Star Trek IV: The Voyage Home*.

Far right: Robert Young and TV daughter Lauren Chapin on the cover of *TV Guide*.

How to Marry a Millionaire
(1958–1959) Syndicated

This TV show was based on a 1953 movie also titled, *How to Marry a Millionaire* starring Marilyn Monroe, Lauren Bacall, and Betty Grable. A cheerful comedy about three sexy New York career girls living in a swank penthouse apartment they can barely afford, and out to snare rich husbands by any scheme they can concoct. Merry Anders (*centre*) played Mike, the ringleader of the group; Barbara Eden (*left*) played Loco, the dim-witted blonde who was so near-sighted she kept walking into walls; and Lori Nelson (*right*) was Greta, the breezy man-hunter.

Top left: The girls live on set, scheming not what to eat, but possibly who to meet.

Bottom left: What chance does this mere male have with three charming and beautiful girls casting their attentions in his direction?

The Tonight Show
(27 September 1954) NBC

This NBC late-night talk show was hosted firstly by
Steve Allen (27 September 1954–25 January 1957),
then Jack Paar (29 July 1957–30 March 1962) and
finally Johnny Carson (1 October 1962–22 May 1992).
A brilliant host and comedian, Carson starred for
30 years in the role.

Below: Johnny Carson on the cover of
TV Guide on 30 July 1966.

The Lawman

(5 October 1958–9 October 1962) **ABC**

With his granite-jaw face and moustache, John Russell *was* Marshall Dan Troop of Laramie, Also starring were Peter Brown as his young deputy, Johnnie McKay; Bek Nelson as Dru Lemp, owner of the Blue Bonnet Café; Barbara Long as Julie Tate, editor of the Laramie newspaper, and Peggie castle as Lily Merrill, proprietor of the Birdcage Saloon.

Left: *The Lawman* cast members (*from left*) John Russell, Peter Brown and Peggie Castle.

Below: John Russell and Peggie Castle on the cover of *TV Times* on 30 September 1961.

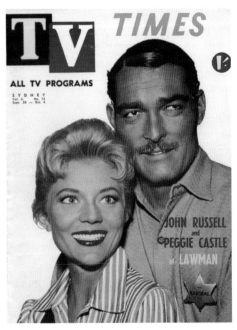

Right: Rosemarie Asturi and Peter Brown in the episode 'The Squatters' in 1961.

Below: Russell and Peter Brown on the cover of *TV Times* on 19 March 1960.

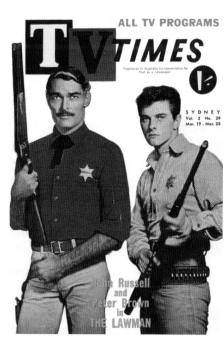

Why Don't They Talk About Haleloke?

TV GUIDE

15¢

COMPLETE LOCAL
PROGRAM LISTINGS
Week of August 14-20

Patti Page

Complete Program Listings, May 11-17, 196?

TV WEEK

That Singers' Singer, PATTI PAGE, Says Luck Is Only 98% of It (Page 12)
Inside in Color: Sammy, the Way-Out Seal, Stars on Walt Disney Show

The Patti Page Show
(1955–1956) Syndicated
(16 June 1956–7 July 1956) **NBC**,
(24 September 1958–16 March 1959) **ABC**

In the 1950s, Patti Page was a bestselling
female artist, hosted several television series
including *The Scott Music Hall*, and also
deputised for Perry Como on his show
in the summer of 1956. The following
year, she also hosted *The Big Record* and, in
1958, *The Oldsmobile Show*. Some of her
hits included, *With My Eyes Wide Open,
I'm Dreaming, Tennessee Waltz, All My Love
(Bolero), I Went to Your Wedding* and *How Much
Is That Doggie in the Window?* Even when rock
and roll became popular in the late 1950s,
Page still maintain her success with hits such
as *Old Cape Cod, Allegheny Moon, A Poor
Man's Rose* and *Hush, Hush, Sweet Charlotte.*

Hancock's Half Hour
(1956–1960)

Tony Hancock starred as Anthony Aloysius St John Hancock, a down-at-heel comedian living in dilapidated lodgings at 23 Railway Cuttings in East Cheam. After debuting on radio in 1954, the popular series began on television in 1956, with only Sid James transferring from radio, although Kenneth Williams and Hattie Jacques each made appearances. Other cast included Liz Fraser, John Le Mesurier, Hugh Lloyd and Arthur Mullard. Hancock was an enormous star in Britain, but sadly his mixture of egotism and self-doubt led to a spiral of self-destructiveness, resulting in suicide in Sydney, Australia, in 1968.

Near left: Sid James on the cover of *TV Times* on 5 October 1961.

Far left: Tony Hancock (*right*) with Sid James (*left*) and Peter Sellers, three brilliant but vastly different British comedians.

The Pat Boone Show
(3 October 1957–23 June 1960) **ABC**
(17 October 1966–30 June 1967) **NBC**

A clean-cut and popular singer of the 1950s, Pat Boone become well known after appearing regularly on Arthur Godfrey's Talent Scouts in 1954. He soon hosted various shows of his own and with his records selling in the millions (*Love Letters in the Sand*) he soon secured his own show. The show was a primetime half-hour variety, featuring the McGuire Sisters and the Mort Lindsey Orchestra. Boone's show in the 1960s was a daytime, half-hour variety and talk show.

Left: Pat Boone surrounded by his four daughters on Father's Day in 1959. They are Cheryl Lynn (*left*) and Linda Lee, while seated on his lap are Laura Gene (*left*) and Deborah Ann.

Below: Nat King Cole, the famed recording artist with the amazing velvet voice, appeared on *The Pat Boone Show*, on 1 October 1959.

Above: Young pioneer Andy Burnett (Jerome Courtland) falls under the spell of Spanish beauty Estrellita (Adele Mara) in Walt Disney's 'The Saga of Andy Burnett' in 1957.

Walt Disney Presents

(27 October 1954–17 September 1961) **ABC**
(24 September 1961–13 September 1981) **NBC**
(26 September 1981–24 September 1983) **CBS**

Walt Disney's television series was one of the most remarkably successful shows in the history of broadcasting. It was aired on all three commercial networks under several different titles, the first primetime anthology series for children and even survived the death of its host and creator. The series premiere telecast, *The Disneyland Story*, in 1954 showed the construction of the park and whetted the curiosity for young viewers. At first, Disneyland was divided into four rotating segments…Frontierland, Fantasyland, Tomorrowland and Adventureland. One of the early favourites was the three Davy Crockett segments, starring Fess Parker with Buddy Ebsen as his sidekick, George Russell. After Disney passed away in 1965, in subsequent seasons there was no opening and closing host, simply voice-over narration.

The Perry Como Show (The Chesterfield Supper Club/ The Kraft Music Hall)
(24 December 1948–4 June 1950) **NBC**
(2 October 1950–24 June 1955) **CBS**
(17 September 1955–12 June 1967) **NBC**

The very popular and talented Perry Como hosted this musical variety show, which Perry usually opened and closed with a song. Some of the regulars included: The Fontane Sisters, Ray Charles Singers, Louis Da Pron Dancers and Peter Gennaro Dancers.

Above: It was always a great night's viewing when two of the country's favourite singing stars, Minday Carson and Perry Como, backed by the Mitchell Ayres' orchestra, came into homes.

Right: *The Perry Como Show*, while known for its many famous guest singers, also showcased the best comedians in the busines...and who was bigger than the legendary Bob Hope, seen here in the 1957 Christmas Special.

Below: Perry Como and friends on the cover of *TV Guide*.

The People's Choice
(6 October 1955–25 September 1958) **NBC**

Jackie Cooper starred as Socrates (Sock) Miller, a government naturalist who became a city councillor in New City, Oklahoma. His job saw him regularly in trouble with Mayor Peoples, which made it interesting as he was his girlfriend Mandy's father. The gimmick for the show, however, was Sock's pet basset hound, Cleo, who made various comments to the viewers. Other cast included: Sock's girlfriend and later his wife, Pat Breslin, who played Amanda (Mandy) Peoples, Paul Maxey as the mayor and Mandy's father, John Peoples, Margaret Irving as Sock's Aunt Gus, Leonid Kinskey as Pierre, Dick Wesson as Rollo and finally the 'talking basset hound' Cleo, who made droll comments on occasions.

Did you know?

Long before his success on television in the 1950s, Jackie was a top box-office movie star as one of the legendary 'Little Rascals' in the early 1930s. He played the role of Jim Hawkins in the 1934 classic film, *Treasure Island*. Later, Jackie also appeared in all four *Superman* movies in the 1970s and 80s, playing the role of Perry White.

Left: Cleo the talking basset hound on the cover of *TV Guide* for the start of the New Year in 1956.

The Real McCoys

(3 October 1957–20 September 1962) **ABC**
(30 September 1962–22 September 1963) **CBS**

Television's first successful rural sitcom, after early misgivings by television executives to whether give it a timeslot, proved a massive hit and was the forerunner for *The Andy Griffith Show* and *The Beverly Hillbillies*. The premise was simple, about a happy-go-lucky West Virginia mountain family who decide to try their luck on a ranch in California's San Fernando Valley. Star of the show was certainly the 63-year-old Walter Brennan as Grandpa Amos McCoy, the meddling old codger with a wheezy voice. Richard Crenna was his grandson, Luke McCoy, Kathy Nolan was Luke's wife Kate; Michael Winkelman played Little Luke McCoy, an orphaned grandson of Amos, Lydia Reed played Hassie, Little Luke's older sister; Tony Martinez as Pepion Garcia, the hired hand, Andy Clyde as George MacMichael, Amos's sometime friend and on other occasions his enemy and Madge Blake as Flora MacMichael, George's sister.

Right: *The Real McCoys'* Richard Crenna, Kathy Noland and Walter Brennan at the breakfast table on set in 1959.

Near right: Walter Brennan and Jane Darwell appear together in *The Real McCoys*.

Far right: Walter Brennan on the cover of *TV Times*.

Alfred Hitchcock Presents/ The Alfred Hitchcock Hour

(2 October 1955–25 September 1960) **CBS**
(27 September 1960–18 September 1962) **NBC**
(20 September 1962–18 September 1964) **CBS**
(5 October 1964–6 September 1965) **NBC**

Alfred Hitchcock entered television in 1955 as host of a half-hour anthology series of mysteries and melodramas. At the beginning of each episode, Hitchcock's silhouette was seen filling the famous line drawing of his profile. The camera would then turn to Hitchcock himself, who would introduce the evening story with a few well-chosen witty remarks. Suspense and surprise endings were the trademarks of the series. Hitchcock reappeared at the end of each show, sometimes to tie up a loose end, sometimes to assure viewers that the killer had been apprehended. In 1962, the show expanded to one hour and was retitled *The Alfred Hitchcock Hour.* Just some of the many stars who made appearances over the ten-year run were: Brian Keith, Claude Rains, Dick York, Joanne Woodward, Steve McQueen, Peter Lorre, Dick Van Dyke, Robert Redford, Peter Fonda.

Did you know?

The opening remarks were filmed in French and German as well as English. Although Hitchcock hosted every episode, he directed only 20 of the over 350 episodes. Alfred Hitchcock drew the caricature of himself featured in the opening credits. He began his film career as an illustrator of title cards for silent movies. You might notice that whenever there was an episode where a 'bad guy' got away with a crime, Hitchcock would say something like, 'Three weeks later the criminal was killed in a car accident' or some other similar demise. The reason was that Hitchcock believed that the evildoers should sometimes get away, just like in real life, but the sponsors had a problem with that. So by stating that they would 'get their due' at some (not too distant) future date, both Hitchcock and the sponsors were happy.

Above: *Alfred Hitchcock Presents*

Left: The brilliant Alfred Hitchcock, who was the master of suspense...

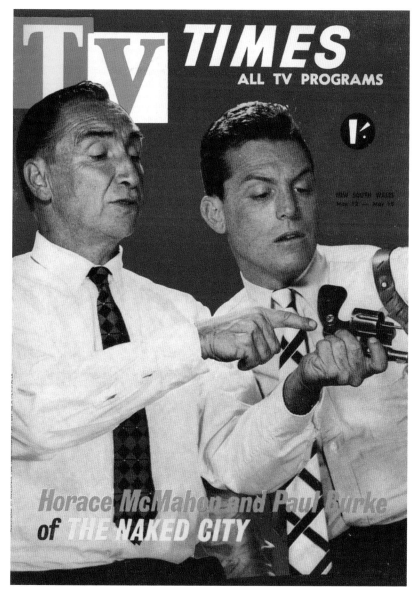

The Naked City

(30 September 1958–29 May 1964) **ABC**

Filmed entirely on location in New York, this popular half-hour crime show initially only ran for one season, before returning after a season's absence in a revamped hour-long format. Gritty reality pervaded the stories, as veteran cop Dan Muldoon and his young sidekick Jim Halloran hunted down the murderers and muggers, petty thieves and swindlers who infested the city's seamy side. The opening season included James Franciscus as the boss, Det. Jim Halloran, John McIntire as Lt. Dan Muldoon and Harry Bellaver as Sgt. Frank Arcaro. Horace McMahon replaced McIntire in March 1959 as Lt. Mike Parker. When the series returned in October 1960, Franciscus was gone, Paul Burke was introduced as Det. Adam Flint and Nancy Malone as Flint's girlfriend, Libby. *Naked City*'s famous tag-line…'There are eight million stories in the Naked City; this has been one of them', was first used in the 1948 film from which the series was derived.

Left: *The Naked City* stars Horace McMahon and Paul Burke on the cover of *TV Times* on 12 May 1962.

The Texan

(29 September 1958–12 September 1960) **CBS**

This was a half-hour western starring Rory Calhoun as Bill Longley, a fast-drawing drifter who made a name for himself throughout the state of Texas. He was a loyal friend, but also a mortal enemy to those who broke the law or hurt people close to him, travelling from town to town to help people in need, with a little romance. Calhoun was also executive producer with Vic Orsatti.

Bachelor Father

(15 September 1957–7 June 1959) **CBS**
(18 June 1959–21 September 1961) **NDC**
(3 October 1961–25 September 1962) **ABC**

Bachelor Father told the story of an unmarried Beverly Hills attorney whose carefree bachelor life is disrupted when his newly orphaned 13-year-old niece came to live with him. John Forsyth played lawyer Bentley Gregg, Noreen Corcoran as niece Kelly Gregg and Sammee Tong as Peter Tong the butler. His clients included many glamorous and available women.

Left: *Bachelor Father* stars (*from left to right*) John Forsythe, Noreen Corcoran and Sammee Tong.

Below: *Bachelor Father*'s John Forsythe and Noreen Corcoran and their pet on the cover of *TV Week* on 9 March 1961.

Did you know?

Linda Evans appeared in one episode as a girlfriend of Kelly. Two decades later, on the series *Dynasty*, she and John Forsyth were man and wife.

Right: John Forsythe and Sandra Warner, one of his many devoted lovely 'attractions' of the show in 1959.

Below: When Sammee Tong (Peter Tong, the butler) and Noreen Corcoran (Kelly Gregg, daughter of Bentley's sister) get together to stress a point, John Forsyth (lawyer Bentley Gregg) has but one choice…to listen.

American Bandstand
(5 August 1957–May 1988) ABC

This was ABC's longest running series. Hosted by Dick Clark, the show featured records, film clips of popular singers and a live audience of local teenagers who danced while the records were played. The show provided the chance for new performers to do their newest hits. Over the years almost every major rock star appeared at least once (two notable exceptions were Elvis Presley and Rick Nelson).

Left: The lovely McGuire sisters (Christine, Phyllis and Dorothy, *left to right*) are flanked by singer Johnny Mathis (*left*) and Dick Clark. Mathis and the McGuire sisters were among the top stars Dick Clark spotlighted in his first hour-long special show, 'The Record Years', on 28 June 1959.

NEW AMERICAN BANDSTAND '65

Did you know?

On the 1957 Thanksgiving show, two New York teenagers who called themselves Tom and Jerry sang their hit record *Hey Schoolgirl*. They are better known today as Paul Simon and Art Garfunkel.

Left: Dick Clark of *New American Bandstand*.

Lassie

(12 September 1954–12 September 1971) **CBS**
(1971–1974) **Syndicated**

Lassie the wonder collie had starred previously in films and on radio. While the role required many various cast changes over the years that followed, Lassie was played by at least six different dogs, all males, while other dogs were substituted for difficult stunts. For the first three seasons of the show Lassie lived with the Millers on their farm and the main cast included Tommy Rettig as Jeff Miller, Jan Clayton as his widowed mum Ellen, George Cleveland as Gramps, Jeff's granddad. After three seasons with Tommy Rettig outgrowing the role, cast changes were needed. Jon Provost came in as Timmy Martin, while Cloris Leachman and Jon Shepodd lasted just one season as Timmy's mum and dad Ruth and Paul. By 1958, June Lockhart and Hugh Reilly (still as Ruth and Paul) came in. Over the following seasons changes evolved and by 1964 Lassie had a new owner when Robert Bray stepped in as Corey Stewart, a forest ranger. With this new role away from farm life, Lassie became involved in a much wider variety of situations. From 1968–1970 Lassie was with a pair of forest rangers (Jed Allan as Scott Turner and Jack de Mave as Bob). During the last few seasons there were no regular humans as Lassie returned to a farm run by Keith Holden (played by Larry Wilcox). While there were many changes throughout this long-running show the one constant was Lassie, a highly intelligent, brave and loyal collie who stole our hearts with her determination to help her masters out of tricky situations.

Did you know?

All the Lassies were actually male dogs.

Right: Lassie, Tommy Rettig, Jan Clayton and George Cleveland in 1955.

Roller Derby

The sport, which sometimes seemed more like a head-bashing free-for-all than a test of athletic skill, combined elements of skating, football, rugby and wrestling. In the early days on TV in 1949 the New York Chiefs were always the home team, playing the San Francisco Bay Bombers or The Mid West Pioneers or others. In later years the sport developed popularity in Australia in the mid 1960s.

Above: Roller derby skaters.

Right: Roller game favourites, the Thunderbirds (*from left to right*) Ronnie Rains, Mannie Servin and Ralphie Valladares during the mid-1960s.

(L to R) Ronnie Rains, Mannie Servin and Ralphie Valladares of the Roller Game

Mr Adams and Eve

(4 January 1957–23 September 1958) **CBS**

Real-life husband and wife pair Howard Duff and Ida Lupino played film-star couple Howard Adams and Eve Adams in *Mr Adams and Eve*, who lived in Beverly Hills. Possible real-life situations were brought to television as fights with the studios bosses, negotiations with their agent, the fun times and no so fun times of their home life were all brought to the mall screen in a light-hearted approach. Alan Reed played J. B. Hafter the studio boss, Hayden Rorke played their agent Steve and Olive Carey was the Adams' housekeeper.

Right: Movie star Eve Adams (Ida Lupino) clutches the new man in her life (Oscar the Academy Award), while husband Howard (Howard Duff) plaintively reminds her of his presence in an episode of *Mr Adams and Eve*.

Below: *Mr Adams and Eve*, starring Ida Lupino and Howard Duff.

Above: Ozzie and Harriet, with the boys Dave (16) and Ricky (13).

Ozzie and Harriet
(10 October 1952–3 September 1966) **ABC**

The Adventures of Ozzie and Harriet was a real family affair, with Ozzie Nelson creating it, directing it, writing in it (together with his brother Don and Bill Davenport and Ben Gershman) and starring in it alongside his wife Harriet and two sons, David and Ricky. Originally a popular radio show from 1944–1954, the television version started in 1952. With their home modelled on their real-life home in Hollywood, this show could also be classed as the real-life family on air, complete with all the adventures we experience with our young children growing up. Ozzie seemed to spend all his time at home or in the yard, while Harriet could usually be found in the kitchen. Some of the other cast members included: Thorny Thornberry played by Don DeFore, Darby played by Parley Baer, Joe Randolph played by Lyle Talbot, Joe's wife, Clara Randolph, played by Mary Jane Croft and Doc Williams played by Frank Cady. David and Ricky, who both became lawyers, also had a number of friends, including Wally Plumstead played by Skip Young, Wally's girlfriend Ginger played by Charlene Salerno, Miss Edwards, who was David and Rick's secretary, played by Connie Harper, while later, David and Ricky's real-life wives, June and Kris, made appearances. In most episodes Ricky and his band would play a tune to close the show, which proved a catalyst for a very successful rock and roll career with *I'm Walkin'*, *Be-Bop Baby*, and *A Teenager's Romance* some of his big hits.

Left: *Ozzie and Harriet's* Ricky Nelson on the cover of *TV Week* on 9 July 1959.

Did you know?

The Nelsons' home on television was modelled after their actual home in Hollywood. Like many other family comedies, Ozzie's (the father's) occupation was never clearly defined. In the episode #160, 'Rick, The Drummer', it was stated that Ozzie had at one time been an orchestra leader with his wife Harriet as the vocalist. That was actually also true during the 1930s in their real lives.

Right: Judging by this article in the 1950s, the Nelson's youngest boy Ricky was not being spoilt with too much spending money.

Below: Dave Nelson checks the qualifications of a pair of beauty-queens, Venita Wolf (*left*) and Marilyn Tindall ('Miss California', 1962) in 'Dave Goes to the Lawyers' Convention' on The *Adventures of Ozzie and Harriet.*

TV'S YOUNGEST COMIC

RICKY NELSON EARNS $1600 WEEKLY
BUT HE GETS ONLY $1.50 TO SPEND . . .

Richard Diamond, Private Detective

(1 July 1957–30 September 1957,
2 January 1958–25 September 1958,
15 February 1959–20 September 1959) **CBS**
(5 October 1959–6 September 1960) **NBC**

Left: Before *The Fugitive*, David Janssen played the title role in *Richard Diamond, Private Detective*. Janssen was cast as a suave private investigator who smokes out a variety of criminals, from high society con men to underworld gamblers.

Below: David Janssen as Richard Diamond on the cover of *TV Times* on 6 August 1960.

Left: The Cleavers (from left to right): Wally (Tony Dow), June (Barbara Billingsley), Ward (Hugh Beaumont) and The Beaver (Jerry Mathers), the quintessential American family.

Below: Jerry Mathers as The Beaver in 1959 then aged 11 years old.

Leave It to Beaver

(4 October 1957–17 September 1958) **CBS**
(2 October 1958–12 September 1963) **ABC**

A family sitcom following the adventures of the young Theodore Cleaver (or The Beaver) played by Jerry Mathers, as well as his family: patient and understanding parents, Hugh Beaumont as Ward Cleaver, and his mum June played by Barbara Billingsley, with his older brother Wally played by Tony Dow. Some of Beaver's mates were Larry (Rusty Stevens), Whitey (Stanley Fafara) and Gilbert (Stephen Talbot), while Wally had Eddie (Ken Osmond) and Lumpy (Frank Bank). The story usually centred about Beaver's well-intentioned efforts, which would go wrong, landing him in trouble. With Beaver just 7 when the series began and older brother Wally just 12, the two showcased many of the differences we encounter as we grow older…Beaver playing games and loving pets, while Wally was starting to get interested in girls as he approached his teenage years.

The Jackie Gleason Show (The Honeymooners)/
Jackie Gleason and his American Scene Magazine

(20 September 1952–22 June 1957, 3 October 1958–2 January 1959, 3 February 1961–24 March 1961,
29 September 1962–12 September 1970) **CBS**

The Honeymooners started as a segment within other programmes and starred Jackie Gleason as
Ralph Kramden. a New York bus driver living in a small apartment with his wife Alice Kramden (played by
Audrey Meadows then later Sheila Macrae) and their upstairs neighbours Ed Norton and his wife Trixie,
played by Art Carney and Joyce Randolph followed by Jane Kean.

Did you know?

When filming in front of a live audience, if Jackie Gleason patted himself on the stomach it was a
sign that he had forgotten his line. In addition to Audrey Meadows and Joyce Randolph, several other
actresses played the roles of Alice and Trixie. Pert Kelton, Sue Anne Langdon and Sheila MacRae played
Alice. Elaine Stritch, Patricia Wilson and Jane Kean played Trixie. Jackie Gleason did not originally
want Audrey Meadows to be cast for the part of Alice Kramden. He thought she was too young and too
pretty. She sent him pictures of herself dressed as a poor housewife and he changed his mind.

Above: Art Carney and Joyce Randolph
as Ed Norton and his wife Trixie,
upstairs neighbours to Ralph Kramden
and Alice in *The Honeymooners*.

Right and below: Dean Martin and Jerry Lewis, an unforgettable comedy team. They first worked together at The 500 Club in Atlantic City in 1946, with their brilliant chemistry realising immediate success on radio, film and finally television. Ten years to the day (25 July 1956) after teaming up, the pair went their own ways and didn't speak to each other until 1976.

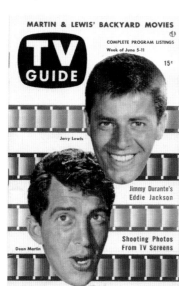

The Life and Legend of Wyatt Earp
(6 September 1955–26 September 1961) **ABC**

Wyatt Earp was unique. Not only was it based on fact but it developed its characters over a period of six years in a continuing story involving politics and family relationships as well as standard western action. Wyatt Earp was played Hugh O'Brien, Bat Masterson was played by Mason Alan Dinehart III, Ben Thompson was played by Denver Pyle and Hal Baylor, Abbie Crandall was played by Gloria Talbot, Doc Holliday was played by Douglas Fowley and Deputy Hal Norton was played by William Tannen.

Did you know?

Despite leading a very dangerous lifestyle, the real Wyatt Earp lived 81 years! He was born in 1848 and died in 1929.

Left: Wyatt Earp played by Hugh O'Brien outside his Marshall's office.

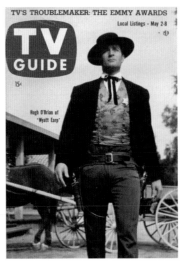

Left: Hugh O'Brien of *Wyatt Earp* on the cover of *TV Guide* on 2 May 1959. The final five episodes of *The Life and Legend of Wyatt Earp* told the story of the famed gunfight at the O.K. Corral between the Earp brothers (Wyatt, Morgan & Virgil) and the Clanton gang.

Left: Steve McQueen as Josh Randall, the star and bounty hunter on *Wanted Dead or Alive* in 1958.

Below: Steve McQueen on the cover of *TV News-Times* on 3 October 1959.

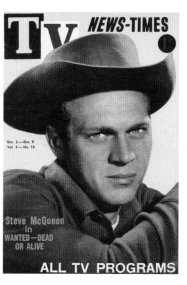

Wanted Dead or Alive

(9 September 1958–29 March 1961) **CBS**

Steve McQueen stars as one of the old west bounty hunters, Josh Randall, who toted an 1892 44/40 centre-fire Winchester carbine that he affectionately referred to as his 'Mare's Leg', a cross between a hand gun and a rifle. A man of few words, he felt little emotion as he chased down targets. For a short while in 1960 Josh had a sidekick in young Jason Nicholls, played by Wright King, before reverting back to riding alone again.

Did you know?

Steve McQueen's movie career was not doing very well when he decided to take the role of Josh Randall. His best-known role to date was in *The Blob* (1958). When the show became a big hit his offers for movie roles returned and that led to his magnificent film career. The role that led to stardom for McQueen was as Vin Tanner in the 1960 film, *The Magnificent Seven*.

The Ed Sullivan Show

(20 June 1948–6 June 1971) **CBS**

Television's longest-running variety show ran on Sunday nights for 23 years. Its host, Ed Sullivan, couldn't sing or dance, but he knew who could, and the list of artists appearing on his show was a who's who of the entertainment world over this period. On camera, Sullivan always seemed ill at ease. He regularly fluffed introductions and wandered around stage during broadcasts. The format of the show remained largely unchanged for its long run, with a typical evening's entertainment including an acrobat, a comic, a recording star or an operatic aria.

Above: The cast of the very first *Ed Sullivan Show* on 20 June 1948, lined up for this group shot. Some of the stars included: Sullivan (*standing forward*), Dean Martin (*right of Sullivan*), Oscar Hammerstein II (*left of Sullivan*), Richard Rodgers (*next to Hammerstein*) and Jerry Lewis (*fifth from left*).

Right: Ed Sullivan with Elvis Presley on *The Ed Sullivan Show* in 1956.

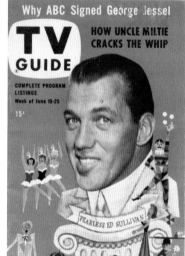

Above: Fabian, the singing idol of the teenagers in June 1959, celebrated the 11th anniversary of *The Ed Sullivan Show* on 21 June 1959.

Above top right: Ed Sullivan and Sid Caesar. A great 'ideas' comic, Caesar was rated the 'comedian of comedians' in the early days of TV.

Above bottom right: Ed Sullivan on the cover of *TV Guide* on 19 June 1953.

Did you know?

The Ed Sullivan Show was nominated for an Emmy for Best Variety Series every year from 1952–1956. It won in 1956 and also won Golden Globes in 1959 and 1960 for Best TV Show!

Bat Masterson

(8 October 1958–21 September 1961) **NBC**

Gene Barry starred as Bat Masterson an ex-lawman who roamed the west. His gimmick was a gold-tipped cane that disguised a sword. A romancer of the ladies, he roamed the west protecting the innocent, while all the time dressed more like a dandy back east rather than He also carried a gun of course.

Did you know?

In real life, Bartley Masterson had been a deputy for Wyatt Earp. You may remember Gene Barry as Captain Amos Burke on the series, *Burke's Law*, as Glenn Howard, on *The Name of the Game,* or as Gene Bradley on *The Adventurer.* Then, in 1994, Gene reprised his role as Amos Burke on a new and updated, *Burke's Law.* The only real difference was that Amos Burke had been promoted from police captain to police chief!

Above: Gene Barry escorts Adele Mara to a theatre in a scene from 'Double Showdown', the premiere episode of the serial, *Bat Masterson*. Barry, starred as the gun-toting, cane carrying Masterson in the serial based on the life of the famous US Marshall, Indian Scout and gunfighter. In this episode Miss Mara portrays beautiful Maria Costa from Mexico, whom Masterson meets en-route to Tombstone.

left: Gene Barry as Bat Masterson on the cover of *TV Times* on July 28, 1960.

Cheyenne
(20 September 1955–13 September 1963) **ABC**

This hour-long western starred Clint Walker as Cheyenne Bodie, drifter of mixed descent. He was a tall and mean hombre, who drifted from job to job, encountering plenty of villains, beautiful girls and the customary gunfights. In the third season *Cheyenne* alternated with *Sugarfoot* and its subsequent history was closely entwined with *Bronco*. By 1958, Walker left the series, but the show continued. Ty Hardin as Bronco Layne starred in the series in the 1958/59 season, as *Cheyenne* again alternated with *Sugarfoot*. By mid-1959 Walker agreed to return to *Cheyenne*, but Hardin had proved popular enough as Bronco to merit his own series. By 1960/61 season episodes of *Cheyenne, Bronco* and *Sugarfoot* were all shown under the *Cheyenne* title.

Left: A sponsor's flyer advertising Clint Walker as Cheyenne on TCN-9 in Australia.

Far left: Clint Walker fights an Indian in a 1958 episode of *Cheyenne*.

Near left: *Cheyenne*'s Clint Walker on the cover of *TV News-Times* on 8 November 1958.

Sugarfoot

(17 September 1957–20 September 1960) **ABC**

An hour-long western starring Will Hutchins as Tom 'Sugarfoot' Brewster, a naive, sarsaparilla-drinking easterner who headed west. His intention was to become a lawyer. He was somewhat inept as a cowboy so he earned the nickname 'Sugarfoot'—one grade lower than a tenderfoot—in the first episode.

Bronco Layne

(20 October 1959–13 September 1960) **ABC**

An hour-long western starring Ty Hardin as Bronco Layne, a loner who drifted across the Texas plains after the American civil war. There were no other regulars but Bronco Layne did encounter plenty of interesting characters during his travels, including Billy the Kid, Jesse James (played by James Coburn) and Wild Bill Hickok.

Below: Will Hutchins as Sugarfoot

Below right: Ty Hardin as Bronco Layne on the cover of *TV Times*.

Did you know?

Sugarfoot aired every other week, alternating with another western series titled, *Cheyenne* for its first two seasons. In its final season, another western titled, *Bronco Layne* was added to the mix and *Sugarfoot* aired every third time in the time slot. Sugarfoot was not the typical tough-guy western lead character. He used his brains and cunning more than he used his fists and weapons.

Man with a Camera
(10 October 1958–29 February 1960) **ABC**

During World War II, Mike Kovac, played by Charles Bronson, had been a combat photographer. Making his living as a freelance professional photographer, he took assignments from newspapers, insurance companies, the police, private individuals, and anyone else who wanted photographers of a particular person or event.

Left: *Man with a Camera*, starring Charles Bronson, surrounded by press photographers of the day.

Below: Cameraman Mike Kovac (Charles Bronson)...'his next photo assignment might take him anywhere from a swank east side supper club to the sinister shadows of a dead-end street to capture on film the story of a city and its people'.

Wagon Train

(18 September 1957–12 September 1962) **NBC**
(19 September 1962–5 September 1965) **ABC**

One of television's most popular westerns, *Wagon Train* was set aboard a wagon train along the trail from Missouri to California in the post-Civil War days. There were many setbacks along the journey, from Indians and the endless deserts, to the towering Rocky Mountains. Each episode was usually a character study, from one of the members of the party or someone encountered along the trip. Ward Bond (*right*) starred as Wagon-master, Major Seth Adams (1957 until his death in 1960). Also featured were Robert Horton as scout Flint McCullough (*left*), Frank McGrath as cook Charlie Wooster, Terry Wilson as Bill Hawks, Denny (Scott) Miller (1961–1963) as scout Duke Shannon, Michael Burns (1963–65) as teenager Barnaby West and Robert Fuller (1963–65) as Cooper, the last scout.

Below: Frank McGrath (*left*) and guest star Tommy Sands in 'The Bob Stuart Story'.

Above left: John McIntire as wagon-master Christopher Hale replaced Ward Bond in 1960. In the September 1962 episode titled 'Madame Sagittarius', McIntire offered to drive Thelma Ritter, when the palmist and medicine woman was shunned by fellow travellers

Above right: Robert Horton on the cover of *TV Times*.

Right: Suzanne Pleshette stars as a dance-hall girl who says her vagabond husband has ruined her life, but refuses help, on *Wagon Train* in 'The Myra Marshall Story'.

Did you know?

Ward Bond started his acting career when one of his fellow football players at USC got him some work as an extra. His college teammate was John Wayne! *Wagon Train* had two wagon-masters during its run. Ward Bond died in November of 1960 and John McIntire took over as the head man in the spring of 1961.

The Red Skelton Show

(30 September 1951–21 June 1953) **NBC**
(22 September 1953–23 June 1970) **CBS**
(14 September 1970–29 August 1971) **NBC**

One of television's most popular comedians, Red Skelton hosted his own show for 20 years! From his pre-television days in vaudeville then radio, Skelton developed many of the characters that he would later bring to television…Junior (the Mean Widdle Kid), Freddie the Freeloader, Clem Kadiddlehopper, George Appleby, Sheriff Deadeye, Willy Lump Lump, Cauliflower McPugg, Cookie the Sailor and many more. A brilliant performer with comedic talent across pantomime, pratfalls and sight gags, his television series proved even more popular than his radio show, bringing to the screen more than just his voice. One of Skelton's writers in the early seasons on CBS was Johnny Carson. Red was a brilliant ad-libber who delighted in breaking up his guest stars.

Did you know?

Comedy writers generally disliked Red Skelton and it's understandable why. Red was determined to write all of his material himself. He felt that he knew his characters better than any other writer and would come up with better material. Before famed comedy writer Sherwood Schwarz would agree to become the head writer for *The Red Skelton Show*, he insisted that a clause be added to his contract that prohibited Red Skelton from discussing scripts with him until he had finished them and handed them in to the production staff. If you've ever seen Red Skelton say, 'Don't blame me, folks, I don't write this stuff', on his show, it's because he often hadn't seen the material until almost time to go on the air!

Left: Red Skelton as Clem Kadiddlehopper, the census taker, getting mixed up in a marriage quarrel with guest stars Gene Barry and Laara Lacey on *The Red Skelton Show*.

Have Gun Will Travel

(14 September 1957–21 September 1963) **CBS**

In *Have Gun Will Travel*, a half-hour western series, Richard Boone starred as Paladin, a loner who lived at the Hotel Carlton in San Francisco. He would offer his professional services as bodyguard, detective, courier etc. His business card bore the image of a chess knight with the words 'Have Gun, Will Travel'. Apart from starring in the role, Boone also directed several episodes and also exercised script and casting approval. The show rated strongly ranking in Nielson's top five in each of its first four seasons.

Did you know?

Paladin used a single-action Colt .44 with a long, rifled barrel. It had a one-ounce trigger pull and was hand-made to his own specifications.

Below: Richard Boone who stars in *Have Gun Will Travel* on the cover of *TV Times* on 20 February 1960.

The Rifleman

(30 September 1958–1 July 1963) **ABC**

Chuck Connors starred as Lucas McCain, a widower trying to raise his young son on a ranch outside the town of North Fork, New Mexico. Unfortunately, Lucas doesn't have much time for ranching, as he is constantly called on to use his prowess with a .44 Winchester rifle to rid North Fork of various undesirables. Johnny Crawford co-stars as his son Mark, while Paul Fix is the town's Marshall, Micah Torrance. Other cast included: Bill Quinn as Sweeney the bartender, Hope Summers as storekeeper Hattie Denton, Joan Taylor as Mille Scott the proprietor of the general store and Pat Blair as Lou Mallory the hotelkeeper.

Below: *Rifleman* father and son Lucas McCain and Mark on the cover of *TV Week* on January 6, 1960.

Did you know?

Chuck Connors played major league baseball for the Chicago Cubs and professional basketball for the Boston Celtics. He was 6'5" tall! Three years before appearing on the Rifleman TV show, young Johnny Crawford was a Mouseketeer on *The Mickey Mouse Club* TV show. Leonid Brezhnev, the leader of the Soviet Union, during a visit to the United States was asked if he'd like to meet any famous Americans. He asked to see Chuck Connors. Apparently, Brezhnev was a big *Rifleman* fan! The two met, became good friends and Chuck Connors later made several trips to Russia!

Right: Chuck Connors and Johnny Crawford who play father and son, Lucas McCain, a widower trying to raise his young son Mark on a ranch outside North Fork.

Below right: Chuck Connors on a break from shooting on the set with a young admirer, complete in his Rifleman t-shirt.

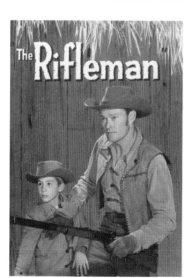

Above: Efrem Zimbalist on the cover of *TV Times* on 9 April 1960.

77 Sunset Strip
(10 October 1958– 9 September 1964) **ABC**

77 Sunset Strip was the prototype for a rash of glamorous private-detective teams in the late 1950s and early 1960s. Efrem Zimbalist Jr. starred as Stu Bailey, and Roger Smith as Jeff Spencer, a couple of private eyes whose business was situated at 77 Sunset Strip in Hollywood. Edd 'Kookie' Brynes co-starred as Gerald Lloyd Kookson III, a car-parking attendant at Dino's Lodge next door. Brynes would later play the part of a detective in 1960. Troy Donahue also co-starred in several 1959 episodes. By 1963, Efrem Zimbalist was the only regular as major changes were brought in. The offices moved from 77 Sunset Strip and a new theme was added, replacing the familiar finger-snapping opener. The success of *77 Sunset Strip* spawned several other serials, such as *Hawaiian Eye* in 1959 and *Surfside Six* in 1960. However none of them were as popular as the original.

Above: The cast of *77 Sunset Strip*. (*From left to right*) Richard Long as Rex Randolph, Efrem Zimbalist Jr. as Stuart Bailey, Jacqueline Beer as Suzanne Fabray, Roger Smith as Jeff Spencer, Louis Quinn as Roscoe and Edward Byrnes as Kookie.

Did you know?

Efrem Zimbalist Jr.'s daughter Stephanie Zimbalist starred as Laura Holt on the TV show, *Remington Steele*.

Rlght: Edd 'Kookie' Byrnes of *77 Sunset Strip*. While it was not planned for Edd Byrnes to have a starring role, the young actor soon dominated the attention of fans. Young female viewers instantly fell in love with his character and young males started imitating him in every way.

Below right: Kookie in his own hot-rod.

Bourbon Street Beat
(5 October 1959–26 September 1960) **ABC**

New Orleans was the setting of this hour-long detective series. It starred Richard Long as Rex Randolph and Andrew Duggan as Cal Calhoun. It also featured Arlene Howell as their receptionist Melody Lee Mercer and Van Williams as their young assistant Kenny Madison. It was the least successful of the detective shows churned out by warner Bros for ABC in the late 1950s and early 1960s.

Above: Stars of the serial Van Williams and Richard Long on set of *Bourbon Street Beat*.

Above top: Andrew Duggan of *Bourbon Street Beat* on the cover of *TV Week* on 28 January 1960.

Above bottom: Richard Long of *Bourbon Street Beat* on the cover of *TV Times* on 28 September 1960.

Colt .45

(18 October 1957–20 September 1960) ABC

A half-hour western starring Wade Preston as government agent Christopher Colt, son of the inventor of the famous Colt revolver most of his missions involved tracking down notorious outlaws, and in the process he had plenty of opportunities to use his famous Colt .45 pistol.

Did you know?

This was one of three different series in which Adam West (*Batman*) appeared as Doc Holliday. The other two were *Lawman* (1958) and *Sugarfoot* (1957).

Right: The man behind the Colt .45, handsome, 6 foot 4 inch Wayde Preston as Christopher Colt.

Below: Chris Colt (Wayde Preston) gets the drop on Jim Rexford (Andrew Duggan) in a scene from the episode 'Judgement Day' in October 1957.

Maverick

(22 September 1957–8 July 1962) **ABC**

Maverick was a western with a sense of humour. 'In the traditional Western, the situation was always serious but never hopeless. In a "Maverick" story, the situation is always hopeless but never serious', producer Roy Huggins stated. Wisecracking ladies' man Brett Maverick, played by James Garner, and brother Bart, played by Jack Kelly, alternated as leads, and sometimes appeared together. Neither of the brothers Maverick was really a hero in the usual sense…they were usually honest in poker but Brett handled a gun rather ineptly and would just as soon slip quietly out of town as face a gunman in an impending showdown.

Left: James Garner leaps over Jack Kelly as Bart Maverick.

Below: *Maverick* star James Garner on the cover of *TV News-Times* on 14 February 1959.

Right: *Maverick*'s James Garner with hotel desk clerk in an episode in 1958.

Below: Roger Moore as cousin Beauregard Maverick and Diana Crawford in a scene from *Maverick* in September 1960.

Above: Raymond Burr and Barbara Hale on the cover of *TV News-Times* on 1 August 1959.

Perry Mason

(21 September 1957–4 September 1966) **CBS**

Perry Mason was one of fiction's most successful criminal lawyers. Raymond Burr played Perry Mason, an aggressive advocate blessed with superb powers of deductive reasoning. Typically, Mason's clients found themselves linked by a change of circumstantial evidence to a murder. However, Mason had the uncanny ability to secure an in-court confession from the real culprit. Other cast members included: Della Street his secretary played by Barbara Hale, Paul Drake, his personal investigator, played by William Hopper, District Attorney Hamilton Burger his perpetual adversary played by William Talman, Lt. Arthur Tragg, the investigating policeman, played by Ray Collins.

Above: Perry Mason (Raymond Burr) and Hamilton Burger (William Talman) discuss a point during one of their many courtroom stoushes. Burger, the District Attorney, who rarely approved of Mason's tactics while defending his clients, had the misfortune to have never won a case against his highly skilled adversary.

Above: Double role…Raymond Burr plays both his usual role as Perry Mason, cross-examining a witness, as well as a man hired to discredit him, in 'The Case of the Dead Ringer' in an episode aired in March 1966.

Did you know?

Raymond Burr originally auditioned for the role of Hamilton Burger, but was chosen for the title role instead.

Right: Hotel clerk Chet Stratton (*right*) meets up with Perry Mason and the always charming Della Street (Barbara Hale) in an episode during the 1959 season.

The Adventures of Zorro
(10 October 1957–24 September 1959) **ABC**

Guy Williams starred as the swashbuckling masked hero in Spanish California in 1820. Returning from Spain at his father's request, Don Diego presented himself as a lazy, foppish aristocrat. Secretly, however, he donned mask and sword and set out to aid the oppressed and foil the schemes of the evil Monastario. His name on these forays was Zorro—for the sign of the 'Z' he cut with his sword—and his loyal manservant was Bernardo, played by Gene Sheldon, who pretended to be a deaf mute to make it easier for him to eavesdrop for his master. Other cast included Henry Calvin as comic foil Sgt. Garcia, Britt Lamond as Capt. Monastario, Don Dimond as Cpl. Reyes and Jolene Brand Anna, who played Maria Verdogo.

Above: Guy Williams and Gilbert Roland cross swords in an episode of *Zorro* in 1958.

Above right top: Williams meets *Zorro* creator Johnston McCulley.

Above right bottom: Series producer Walt Disney and Guy Williams as Zorro.

Did you know?

Zorro was shown in South America throughout the 1960s and 1970s. When Guy Williams travelled to Argentina in 1973, he was feted as the hero 'El Zorro'. He later emigrated there, living outside Buenos Aires until his death in 1989, aged 65.

Gunsmoke

(10 September 1955–1 September 1975) **CBS**

Gunsmoke introduced the 'adult western' to television, and began an enormous wave of 'horse operas' to TV over the ensuing years. While there had been other westerns before such as *The Lone Ranger* and *Annie Oakley*, *Gunsmoke* was the first one oriented towards adult audiences. Within a few years there were more than 30 such shows on the air at one time! Some favourites were *Bronco, Have Gun Will Travel, Maverick, Rawhide, The Rifleman, Wagon Train* and *Wanted Dead or Alive.*

James Arness starred as Marshall Matt Dillon in Dodge City, Kansas. Amanda Blake was Kitty Russell, owner of the Long Branch saloon, Dennis Weaver was Chester B. Goode, Dillon's deputy and Milburn Stone was Doc Adams. In 1962, Burt Reynolds joined the show as Quint Asper, a half-breed blacksmith, while in 1964 Dennis Weaver left and was replaced by Ken Curtis as Festus Hagen. By the third season the show had become the number-one-rated series, which it held for four seasons. Starting as a half-hour show by 1961 it expanded to an hour.

Left: The cast (*from left to right*): Milburn Stone as Doc Adams, James Arness as Marshall Matt Dillon, Amanda Blake as Kitty Russell and Ken Curtis as Festus Hagen.

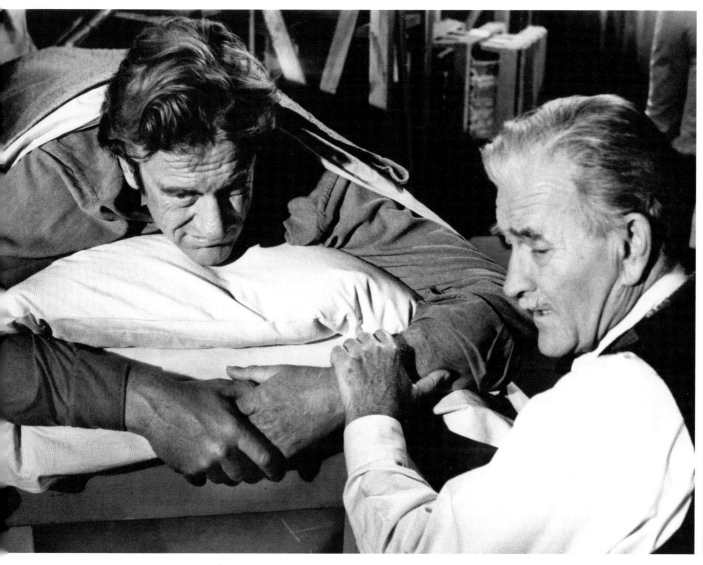

Above: Marshall Matt Dillon, played by James Arness, is critically wounded by bandits and Milburn Stone, as Doc Adams, faces the difficult decision of whether to operate or not, in Gold Train, a three-part story that was aired in November 1971.

Above right top: James Arness as Marshall Matt Dillon.

Above right bottom: Dennis Weaver as Chester. Weaver broke the golden rule of television: he left a top-rating series to forge his own career. But he went on to have a long and successful career in film (*Duel*, 1971) and television (*McCloud*, 1970-77).

Did you know?

Rex Koury had so little time to pen the theme song that he hastily scribbled it while in the bathroom. It was originally written for *Gunsmoke* when it was a radio show and later adapted for TV. The gunfight between Matt Dillon and an unknown gunman that opened every episode was shot on the same street as that which was used in *High Noon* (1952). James Arness is the brother of actor Peter Graves (Jim Phelps in *Mission Impossible*).

The Swinging Sixties saw a huge upheaval in the world and dramatically altered the landscape of television. More liberated thinking, greater expectations and more disposable income brought with it changes in all avenues of our lives and had a profound effect on our entertainment expectations. Money talks and television was listening, now becoming a serious business with the stakes much higher. Success was demanded and shows came and went, with only the best surviving. We were served more instantaneous news reports with video tape allowing the viewer to be there 'live'. The world was getting smaller. The saccharine sweet Fifties outlook on life was replaced with a more edgy reality to television. Story-lines were more complex and colour TV created greater opportunities and more realism. A new wave of shows and stars hit the screens: The Beatles and The Rolling Stones, *The Untouchables*, *The Twilight Zone*, *Bonanza and The Virginian*, *Peyton Place and Coronation Street*, *Surfside Six and Hawaiian Eye*, *The Munsters and Green Acres*, *General Hospital* and *Days of Our Lives*, *Car 54 Where Are You* and *The Dick Van Dyke Show*, *Combat* and *Star Trek*…what a decade!

Left: The Rolling Stones performing on *Shindig*, a musical variety series which ran on ABC from September 1964 to January 1966.

1960s

The Andy Williams Show

(2 July 1957–5 September 1957) **NBC**
(3 July 1958–25 September 1958) **ABC**
(7 July 1959–22 September 1959) **CBS**
(27 September 1962–3 September 1967) **NBC**
(20 September 1969–17 July 1971) **NBC**
(1976 and 1977) **Syndicated**

Smooth-voiced popular singer Andy
Williams starred in a number of variety
shows in the late 1950s through to the
early 1970s. Big-name guest stars appeared
along with a large number of regulars.
His chief backup act was a quartet of
talented youngsters discovered by Williams
performing at Disneyland. They were
the Osmond Brothers. He later hosted a
syndicated half-hour musical variety series
during the mid-1970s with a similar format.

Left: Jack Benny, Andy Williams and
Janet Leigh on the season premiere
of the *The Andy Williams Show* on
5 October 1964.

Above: Andy Williams (*left*) joins his brothers to reform the
noted Williams Brothers singing group on 11 December 1963.
On this night the finale included Andy's wife Claudine Longet,
14 other members of the Williams family and guest star
Fred MacMurray.

The Ed Sullivan Show
(20 June 1948–6 June 1971) **CBS**

Left: Nancy Sinatra singing her biggest hit from 1966, and possibly of all-time *These Boots are Made for Walkin'*.

Bottom: Ed Sullivan with famed mother and daughter team, Liza Minelli (*left*) and Judy Garland (*right*) in the early 1960s. Above them (*centre*) are Dean Martin and Jerry Lewis on the very first *Sullivan Show* on 20 June 1948. Then in the 1960s their offspring followed in their footsteps, with Gail Martin (*above left*) and Gary Lewis (*above right*) making their appearances on the programme.

Left: In 1964, 73 Million households were watching *The Ed Sullivan Show* to see the first US nationwide appearance of The Beatles! For the baby boomer generation *The Ed Sullivan Show* showcased breakthrough performances for some of the greatest singers and bands of the day...Elvis Presley, The Beatles, The Beach Boys, The Rolling Stones, The Supremes, The Jackson 5, The Mamas & The Papas and The Lovin' Spoonful to name just a few.

Did you know?

When *The Ed Sullivan Show* ended in 1971, it was not due to falling ratings. CBS simply decided to 'modernise' its line-up and felt that the show appealed mostly to older viewers.

Adventures in Paradise
(5 October 1959–1 April 1962) **ABC**

Gardner McKay (*left*) a virtual unknown, rose to stardom as Adam Troy in this adventure story based very loosely on James Michener's book of the same title. Troy was captain of the Tiki, an 85-foot long schooner which sailed the warm waters of the South Pacific. The first network show set in the South Pacific, it was one of the few successful series set outside of the United States.

Did you know?

The 'Tiki' was built at Wollongong on the southern coast of New South Wales (Australia) prior to 1920.

Far left: The 1961 episode, 'Captain Butcher' Jim Benson (John Anderson, *right*) has two South Seas skippers, Adam Troy and Arthur Butcher (Alan Hale), bidding to ship his cargo.

Near left: Gardner McKay on the cover of *TV Times*.

Near left. Dennis' dad Henry Mitchell was selected from a final three (*seen here*) and was played by Herbert Anderson (*bottom right*), while his wife Alice was played by Gloria Henry.

Near left: Dennis the Menace (Jay North) and exasperated neighbour Mr Wilson (Joseph Kearns) on the cover of *TV Times* on 10 March 1962.

Dennis the Menace
(4 October 1959–22 September 1963) **CBS**

Above: Hank Ketcham's mischievous cartoon character made a successful transition to television in this prime-time series which ran for 146 half-hour episodes. Jay North got the part of Dennis the Menace after auditioning along with more than 500 others. After *Dennis the Menace* ended, North got the lead role in the movie, *Maya* (1966) and in the short-lived TV show of the same name. He supplied the voice for cartoon characters in the late 1960s, but starring roles on television and film disappeared.

Did you know?

The inspiration for the comic strip came to Hal Ketcham when his wife once remarked, 'Our son, Dennis, is a menace'.

The Donna Reed Show
(24 September 1958–3 September 1966) ABC

At the centre of this family comedy were Donna Stone, her husband Alex and their teenage kids. The adventures of the Stone family were similar to those of other television families but it had a wholesome quality that endeared it to audiences. *The Donna Reed Show* starred (*from left to right*): Shelley Fabares as daughter Mary Stone, Paul Petersen as son Jeff Stone, Carl Betz as Alex Stone and Donna Reed as Donna Stone.

Did you know?

The Donna Reed Show was the first family-oriented situation comedy where the mother was the star of the show. The series was produced by Tony Owen, who also happened to be Donna Reed's husband.

Right: Donna Reed, who debuted in the film *The Get-Away* in 1941, finished her movie and television career in 1984–85 season playing Miss Ellie Ewing Farlow in *Dallas*. Appearing in over 40 films, she won the 1953 Academy Award for Best Supporting Actress as Lorene Burke in *From Here to Eternity*. She also was nominated for an Emmy in four successive years (1959–1962 inclusive) for her role in *The Donna Reed Show*, before finally winning in 1963.

Rawhide

(9 January 1959–4 January 1966) **CBS**

Rawhide took its regular performers back and forth across the country as organisers and runners of communal cattle drives. The constant travelling allowed the series to tell stories of people met along the way and those who joined the regulars in transit. Gil Favor (*right*) played by Eric Fleming was the trail boss, while his second in command was Rowdy Yates played by Clint Eastwood (*centre*).

Did you know?

While visiting a friend at CBS studios, a studio executive saw Clint Eastwood and thought he looked like a cowboy and recommended him to *Rawhide*'s producers. Although Eric Fleming was the show's star, Eastwood was the breakout star (Eric Fleming drowned tragically on film location in Peru in 1966). DVD packages released years later prominently featured Eastwood, due to his later fame.

Far left: *Rawhide*'s Clint Eastwood on the cover of *TV Week* on 31 December 1959.

Near left: As the advert said, 'You'll thrill to this hour-long adventure series as man and beast struggle for survival on the greatest cattle drive in history'.

The Detectives
(16 October 1959–22 September 1961) **ABC**
(29 September 1961–21 September 1962) **NBC**

Set in New York, with Robert Taylor starring as Matt Holbrook, a humourless, hard-nosed doggedly effective police captain who led a team of plainclothes detectives. The cast originally included Tige Andrews as Lt. Johnny Russo, Lee Farr as Lt. Jim Conway and Russell Thorsen as Lt. Otto Lindstrom.

Left: With Lt. Johnny Russo (Tige Andrews *at right*) and another detective (Dale Van Sickle *at left*) looking on, Captain Matt Holbrook (Robert Taylor) tackles mobster Nick Modesto who was believed dead in the second season premiere titled 'The New Man', which aired on 16 September 1960.

Below: *The Detectives'* Robert Taylor on the cover of *TV Week* on 10 October 1959.

Right: The beautiful Donna Douglas with Mark Goddard in 1960. Goddard joined the show as Detective Sgt. Chris Ballard in season two, replacing Lee Farr, and later found fame on *Lost in Space* (1965–68). Donna Douglas had earlier guest-starred in episodes of *Bachelor Father* and *US Marshall* in 1959 and would eventually go on to star as Elly May Clampett in *The Beverly Hillbillies* (1962–1971).

Below: Adam West (later of *Batman* fame) joined the cast during the third season and played Sgt. Steve Nelson (1961–1962). In this season the show increased from 30 to 60 minutes and was retitled 'Robert Taylor's Detectives'.

The Many Loves of Dobie Gillis

(29 September 1959–18 September 1963) **CBS**

Dwayne Hickman starred as Dobie Gillis (*left*), the confused romantic American teenager who was always trying to work out what he wanted from life. Bob Denver (*right*) co-starred as Maynard G. Krebs, his carefree beatnik friend, who shuddered whenever the word 'work' was mentioned. If Dobie wasn't at the malt shop trying to impress some young, gorgeous girl, he could be found seated beneath a replica of Rodin's *The Thinker*, trying to explain his mixed-up reasoning to the viewer. Other cast included Frank Faylen as Dobie's father, Herbert T. Gillis, who owned the grocery store over which they lived, and Florida Friebus as Dobie's mother, Winifred Gillis. The remaining main players included Sheila James as Zelda Gilroy (*centre*), Tuesday Weld as Thalia Menninger, Stephen Franken as Chatsworth Osborn Jr., Doris Parker as Mrs Chatsworth Osborn, William Schallert as Mr Pomfret and, pre-movie stardom, Warren Beatty as Milton Armitage.

Did you know?

This show was one of the influences in the development of the Hanna-Barbera cartoon *Scooby Doo, Where Are You?* (1969). The character of Fred Jones was based on Dobie Gillis, Velma Dinkley on Zelda Gilroy, Daphne Blake on Thalia Menninger and Norville 'Shaggy' Rogers on Maynard G. Krebs.

Right: Olive Sturgess and Dwayne Hickman in June of 1958.

Below: In this episode, Dobie Gillis is pictured with the lovely Thalia Menninger (played by Tuesday Weld) while the waitress is the very funny character actress Kathleen Freeman (*The Blues Brothers*, 1980).

The Untouchables
(15 October 1959–10 September 1963) **ABC**

Set in Chicago during the 1930s, this hour-long crime
show was based on the real life exploits of Eliot Ness and
his squad of Treasury agents, nicknamed 'The Untouchables'.
A violent series for the times, the show received much
criticism, especially from Italian-American civic groups, with
constant use of Italian-surnamed gangsters. In later episodes
there was a diversification of villains, and by 1963 virtually
every ethnic group had been represented. Other criticism
came from the US Bureau of Prisons, which objected to
the portrayal of prison officials in certain episodes involving
Al Capone. The show was narrated by journalist Walter
Winchell. Robert Stack starred as Eliot Ness, Jerry Paris
played Marvin Flaherty, Nicholas Georgiade played Rossi,
Anthony George played Allison, Abel Fernandez played
Youngfellow, Paul Picerni played Hobson and Steve London
was Rossman. Some of the guest villains included Neville
Brand as Al Capone, Bruce Gordon as Frank Nitti and
Clu Gulagher as 'Mad Dog' Col Caan.

Right: In the episode 'A Fist of Five' in December 1962,
Lee Marvin made his third and final guest appearance
on the series. Some of the other major motion picture and
television guest stars to appear in the series also included
Charles Bronson, Robert Duvall, Peter Falk, Anne Francis,
Brian Keith, Vic morrow, Barry Morse, Leonard Nimoy,
Robert Redford, Telly Savalas, and Barbara Stanwyck.

Did you know?

Hollywood actors Van Johnson, Van Heflin and Cliff Robertson were offered the role as Eliot Ness but turned it down, and Robert Stack made the role his own. Some other famous stars who were considered for the role included Jack Lord (*Hawaii Five-0*) and Fred MacMurray (*My Three Sons*).

Right: *The Untouchables*. (*Left to right*) Abel Fernandez as Agent William Youngfellow, Nicholas Georgiade as Agent Enrico 'Rico' Rossi, Robert Stack as Eliot Ness and Paul Picerni as Agent Lee Hobson.

Near right: Ma Barker (Claire Trevor) and sons Lloyd (Adam Williams) and Fred (Joe Di Reda), outfitted in armoured vests fashioned in the 1930s, get ready for a last-ditch stand in their Florida bungalow in 'Ma Barker and Her Boys'.

Far right: Barbara Nichols was a frequent guest star on many television series during the 1950s and 60s. The leggy flapper appeared in two episodes of *The Untouchables*, as Brandy LaFrance in the premiere episode of 'The Empty Chair', and later as Barbara Ritchie.

131

Twilight Zone

(2 October 1959–14 September 1962),
(3 January 1963–18 September 1964) **CBS**

Right Rod Serling, creator, writer and host
of the original *Twilight Zone* series. One
of television's most popular science fiction
anthology series, Serling introduced each show
with the words: 'There is a fifth dimension,
beyond that which is known to man. It is a
dimension as vast as space and as timeless
as infinity. It is the middle ground between
light and shadow, between science and
superstition, and it lies between the pit of a
man's fears and the summit of his knowledge.
This is the dimension of imagination. It is an
area which we call the Twilight Zone'.

Above: Dennis Weaver (*Gunsmoke*) made
a guest appearance on the 1961 episode
'Shadow Play', as a man convicted of murder.
All episodes during the five original series were
filmed in black and white.

The Roaring Twenties

(15 October 1960–21 September 1962) **ABC**

An hour-long drama serial that deals with reporters working for the *New York Record,* covering crime stories. Dorothy Provine stars as Pinky Pinkham, a singer at the Charleston Club, while the reporters are Donald May as Pat Garrison, Rex Reason as Scott Norris and John Dehner as Duke Williams, while Mike Road played Police Lieutenant Joe Switoski.

Right: Donald May as Pat Garrison and Dorothy Provine as Pinky Pinkham in the episode 'No Exit', aired in 1961. Set in New York during the 1920s, this hour-long adventure series was less violent than *The Untouchables,* but also was less popular.

Bonanza

(12 September 1959–16 January 1973) **NBC**

Bonanza was typical of the 'property western' that dominated the genre during the 1960s. It told the story of the Cartwrights who owned the property The Ponderosa. Canadian actor Lorne Greene was Ben Cartwright, a three-time widower, who had a son to each wife. Pernell Roberts was the eldest son Adam, Dan Blocker was 'Hoss' and Michael Landon was youngest son Little Joe. It was second only to *Gunsmoke* as the longest running western. Even after Pernell Roberts quit the series in 1965 the show continued to rate well.

Below: The Cartwright family gathers around the family dinner table. *Bonanza* was not a traditional shoot-em-up western. It relied more on the relationships between the principals and the stories of the characters played by weekly guest stars than it did on violence.

Did you know?

At first, NBC wanted established stars for the cast of *Bonanza*. However, producer David Dortort understood that this 'new' medium of television would create its own stars. The TV show was not an immediate success in its Saturday night timeslot, and the only thing that actually kept the show alive for the first two years was that it was one of the few series shown in colour. RCA owned NBC and wanted *Bonanza*'s beautiful colourful vistas to sell their new line of colour televisions. When the show was moved to Sunday nights, its ratings then improved dramatically. *Bonanza* was the most globally broadcast show ever. It was aired in every nation on Earth that had a single TV station!

Right: Dan Blocker portrays Hoss Cartwright. Blocker, a giant of a man, was also a onetime football lineman for Sul Ross State College, Alpine, Texas and stood six feet four and weighed 295 pounds. Blocker's sudden death during the summer of 1972 led to the show's cancellation halfway through its 14th season (1972–73).

Near right: The Cartwright family were a formidable sight when pushed too far.

Far right: The cast on the cover of *TV Times*.

Coronation Street

(9 December 1960–)

The longest running soap opera in the world first aired in December 1960 and now has over 8,300 episodes at the time of publication. Devised in 1960 by writer Tony Warren at Granada Televison in Manchester, the story-lines follow the people in their terraced houses, café, corner shop, newsagents, factory and the Rovers Return pub. The original cast included Violet Carson, who played Ena Sharples, self-proclaimed moral voice of Coronation Street, Patricia Phoenix (Elsie Tanner) and Doris Speed (Annie Walker the landlady of the Rovers, Return). The three remained with the show for more than 20 years.

Above: *Coronation Street* cast from the early days in 1970. Many happy returns at the Rovers as it's drinks all-round and the folk of Coronation Street join together to raise their glasses to celebrate the 1000th show. Standing at the back (*from left*): Cyril Turpin, Jack Walker, Betty Turpin, Annie Walker, Valerie Barlow, Audrey Fleming, Hilga Ogden, Dickie Fleming, Ken Barlow, Dot Greenhalgh. Standing in front: Stan Ogden and Elsie Tanner. And seated at the table (*from left*): Minnie Caldwell, Ena Sharples, Emily Nugent.

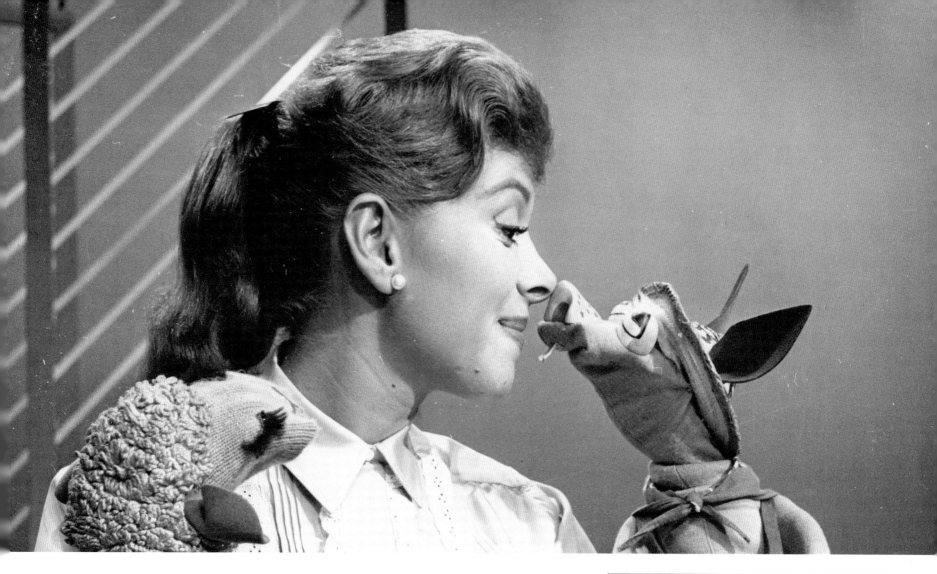

The Shari Lewis Show

(1 October 1960–28 September 1963) **NBC**

Shari Lewis and her puppets, Lamb Chop, Hush Puppy and Charlie Horse starred in this Saturday morning show. Also featured were Jackie Warner as Jum-Pup, Ronald Radd as Mr Goodfellow and Clive Russell.

Above: Shari Lewis with her puppets Lamb Chop and Charlie Horse. Shari was a ventriloquist, puppeteer and an accomplished musician as well as a children's television show host and author with over 60 books to her credit.

Right: Shari Lewis, Lamb Chop and the Mailman. Lewis won 12 Emmy Awards during her career.

Surfside Six

(3 October 1960–24 September 1962) **ABC**

Surfside Six was a cookie-cutter copy of *77 Sunset Strip*. A trio of sexy, young private detectives lived in Miami and spent much of their time with beautiful women. *Surfside Six* was the Miami telephone number that included the number of the houseboat that served as both home and office. Pictured are Margarita Sierra as Cha Cha O'Brien, Troy Donahue as Sandy Winfield II, Lee Patterson as Dave Thorne, Diane McBain as Daphne Dutton and Van Williams as Kenny Madison.

Did you know?

ABC produced detective series with hip characters set in different trendy locales…*Bourbon Street Beat* was set in New Orleans during the 1959–1960 season, *77 Sunset Strip* in Los Angeles from 1958–1964 and *Hawaiian Eye* in Hawaii from 1959–1963. Each series was filmed on the same studio back lot in LA, which made it easy to crossover plots and characters from one show to another.

Right: Ric Roman (Shreiner) has Van Williams (Ken Madison) in a spot of bother in the episode 'Local Gril'.

Above: The cast (*left to right*): Troy Donahue as Sandy Winfield II, Margarita Sierra as Cha Cha O'Brien, Lee Patterson as Dave Thorne, Diane McBan as Daphne Dutton and Van Williams as Ken Madison.

Right: The original *Surfside 6* logo.

Checkmate

(17 September 1960–19 September 1962) **CBS**

Sebastian Cabot starred as Dr Carl Hyatt, theoretician and criminologist. He tried not only to solve crimes but also to prevent them.

Left: *Checkmate*, starring Sebastian Cabot as Dr Carl Hyatt, a college professor who is employed as an adviser for a private detective agency in San Francisco.

Below: The other private eyes who comprised Checkmate Inc. were Tony George (*centre*) as Don Corey and Doug McClure (*right*) as Jed Sills. In most of their cases they tried to protect the lives of people who had been threatened or who suspected they were possible targets of criminals.

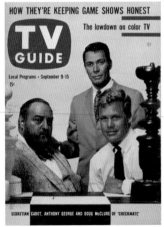

The Champions
(1968–69) UK

Above: This cult UK science-fiction series *The Champions*, (1968–1969) portrayed a group of spies with superhuman abilities, a premise revised by the series, *Heroes*, in 2006. Pictured are Stuart Damon as Craig Stirling, William Gaunt as Richard Barrett and Alexandra Bastedo as Sharron Macready.

Redcap
(17 October 1964–25 June 1966) UK

Right: Popular English actor John Thaw In 1964. He starred in two series of *Redcap*, playing military policeman Sergeant John Mann.

Hawaiian Eye

(7 October 1959–10 September 1963) **ABC**

Set in Honolulu, *Hawaiian Eye* was a detective show featuring (*from left to right*), Robert Conrad as Tom Lopaka, Anthony Eisley as Tracy Steele and Connie Stevens as Cricket Blake. Base of their operations was a poolside office at the Hawaiian Village Hotel.

Right: *Hawaiian Eye*'s Poncie Ponce as colourful cabbie Kazuo Kim on the cover of *TV Times*.

TV TIMES
ALL TV PROGRAMMES

PONCIE PONCE

142

Above: Connie Stevens as Cricket Blake in the Warner Bros. series.

Did you know?

The character Tom Lopaka was originally supposed to be half Polynesian, but there were no big name stars available with that ethnicity. Robert Wagner was offered the role but turned it down because he wanted to pursue his movie career. Wagner recommended his buddy Robert Conrad for the role. Conrad had been looking for work for about a year and spent a lot of time at the beach. His dark tan gave him the perfect look for a suave guy living in Hawaii, and he was given the role.

Above: Robert Conrad (*left*) in his pre *Wild, Wild West* days starred as Tom Lopaka, a partner with Tracy Steele (played by Anthony Eisley) in a detective agency and private security firm located in Honolulu.

Hazel

(28 September 1961–9 September 1965) **NBC**
(13 September 1965–5 September 1966) **CBS**

Hazel was one of only a handful of successful
television series based on a comic strip. Shirley Booth
(*left*) was brilliant as Hazel Burke, the maid for the
Baxter family, with a habit for getting involved in
other people's business. Don Defore (*right*) played
George Baxter, a successful lawyer, Whitney Blake
as his wife Dorothy and Bobby Buntrock as their son
Harold. When the series changed networks in 1965
(and George and Whitney were written out of the
script transferring to the Middle East on work), Hazel
went to work for George's brother Steve (Ray Fulmer),
his wife Barbara (Lynn Borden) and daughter Suzie
(Julia Benjamin). Harold stayed on in the cast, living at
his uncle's place while his parents were overseas.

Far left: *Hazel* star Shirley Booth in a pensive moment
on the set of the show.

Near left: Shirley Booth, who was primarily a theatre
actress, made her debut on Broadway in 1925
opposite Humphrey Bogart. She won a Tony Award
as Lola Delaney in her acclaimed role in the drama
Come Back, Little Sheba, and the Academy Award
and Golden Globe Award for Best Actress reprising
her role in the 1952 film version. She also won two
Emmy Awards in her role as *Hazel*.

144

Kennedy and Nixon Debates
1960

Above and right: Senator John F. Kennedy and Vice-President Richard Nixon, with moderator Howard K. Smith, met in the first televised presidential debate in 1960. Television played an important role in deciding the presidential race, with audiences connecting with the youthful, good-looking Kennedy while former Vice-President Richard Nixon came across as nervous and shallow.

Ben Casey
(2 October 1961–21 March 1966) **ABC**

Vince Edwards starred as Ben Casey, a surly, good-looking resident neurosurgeon at County General Hospital.

'Man, woman, birth, death, infinity…' The opening words of *Ben Casey*, a medical series about an intense but idealistic young surgeon. Vince Edwards (*right*) as Casey became an instant heartthrob with the female audience. Some of the regulars included Sam Jaffe as Dr David Zorba, chief of neurosurgery, Bettye Ackerman as anaesthesiologist Dr Maggie Graham, Harry Landers as Dr Ted Hoffman, Nick Dennis as orderly Nick Kanavaras, Jeanne Bates as Nurse Wills and Franchot Tone as Dr Freeland.

Did you know?

In reflecting on how he got the idea for Ben Casey, series creator James E. Moser said, 'One day I was walking through Los Angeles General Hospital and I came upon a redheaded neurosurgeon. He was snapping into a telephone, "Damn it. Stop having hysterics!" I knew that I had found a new type hero for a medical TV show'.

Above: Actress Tuesday Weld and Vince Edwards in a scence from a 1963 episode of Ben Casey..

Right. Bettye Ackerman and Vince Edwards on the cover of *TV Times*. In real life Ackerman was married to her *Ben Casey* co-star Sam Jaffe (thirty years her senior). The pair remained happily married until Jaffe's passing in 1984, aged 93!

Car 54 Where Are You?

(17 September 1961–8 September 1963) **NBC**

Created by Nat Hiken, *Car 54* was the first sitcom about police officers. The large cast included Joe E. Ross as Officer Gunther Toody (*left*), Fred Gwynne as his partner Officer Francis Muldoon (*centre*), Beatrice Pons as Lucille Toody (Gunther's wife), Al Lewis as Office Schnauzer, Charlotte Rae as Mrs Schnauzer and Paul Reed as Captain Block (*right*). Located in the 53rd Precinct of New York, Officers Toody and Muldoon encountered more comedy than crime.

Below left: Al Lewis as Officer Leo Schnauzer played by Al Lewis. Lewis also had a PhD in child psychology from Columbia University! He ran for Governor of the state of New York for the Green Party in 1998! Al is probably best known as 'Grampa' on the series, *The Munsters* (1964) where he also worked with Fred Gwynne. He later opened a restaurant in New York City called, 'Grampa's'!

Below right: Fred Gwynne and Joe E. Ross off camera with Phil Silvers of *Sergeant Bilko* fame and both show's brilliant creator Nat Hiken.

Did you know?

The patrol car looked identical to those used by real-life New York City police, but only because the show was filmed in black and white. The car was actually painted red and white to distinguish itself from real police during the shooting, all of which was done on location.

The Andy Griffith Show
(3 October 1960–1 April 1968) **CBS**

The small town of Mayberry, North Carolina was the setting of this highly successful homespun sitcom. Sheriff Andy Taylor played by Andy Griffith (*left*) was a widower with a young son, Opie played by Ronnie Howard (*centre*). They lived with Andy's Aunt Bee, played by Frances Bavier. Andy's deputy was his cousin Barney Fife played by Don Knotts (*right*), the most inept, tense deputy sheriff ever seen on television. Since there was practically no crime in Mayberry, the stories revolved mostly around the personal relationships of its citizens. Other cast members included Jim Nabors as Gomer Pyle, George Lindsey (Goober Pyle), Howard McNear (Floyd Lawson), Otis Campbell (Hal Smith) and Betty Lynn as love interest Thelma Lou.

Below: Andy Griffith on the cover of *TV Guide*.

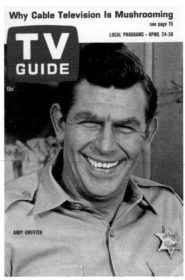

Above: *The Andy Griffith Show* shooting the show's
memorable opening credits scene with Andy and a very
young Opie going fishing.

Did you know?

Andy Griffith was born in a small North Carolina
town named Mount Airy, and he used it as the basis
for the fictitious town of Mayberry.

Right: *The Andy Griffith Show.*
(*From left to right*) Don Knotts,
Andy Griffith and Jim Nabors.

The Avengers

(28 March 1966–15 September 1969) **ABC**

The Avengers was pure British escapist television, centred on the suave and proper British secret agent, Jonathan Steed played by Patrick Macnee. After a few episodes he was joined by his jump-suited female partner Emma Peel, played by Diana Rigg. The missions involved all types of diabolical genius who in many cases were attempting world domination, thwarted by the 'oh so clever Steed'. Macnees's original partner on the British version was Honor Blackman. By March 1968, Steed had a new partner, the younger and voluptuous Linda Thorson who played Tara King replaced Rigg. By 1976, the show was resurrected as *The New Avengers*, with agents Purday (played by Joanna Lumley) and Mike Gambit (played by Gareth Hunt) supporting Steed.

Did you know?

Diana Rigg was the first person ever to perform Kung Fu in a television series. Although his spy work was very dangerous, John Steed was only slightly hurt in three episodes and knocked unconscious in six! That's not too shabby for a 161-episode run!

Above: *The Avengers*; Dianna Rigg and Patrick Macnee.

The Defenders
(16 September 1961–9 September 1965) **CBS**

This high-quality series about a father-and-son defence team attracted much controversy, as well as much critical acclaim. The show regularly dealt with such sensitive issues as euthanasia, abortion, blacklisting and civil unrest. Even more unusual was the fact that the defenders occasionally lost a case. The show starred E. G. Marshall as Lawrence Preston with co-star Robert Reed as his Ivy League son, Kenneth Preston. The two-part pilot also featured Ralph Bellamy and William Shatner. Other cast members included: Polly Rowles as their secretary, Helen Donaldson then later Joan Hackett as Ken's girlfriend and social worker Joan Miller. Among the many guest stars who appeared were Gene Hackman (3 appearances), Martin Sheen, James Farentino, Jon Voight and Ossie Davis.

Above: E. G. Marshall as Lawrence Preston (*left*) and William Shatner who guest starred in various roles in the series.

Right: Robert Reed and E. G. Marshall, as father and son defence attorneys who specialised in legally complex cases, on the cover of *TV Times*.

151

Left: Lucille Ball and Gale Gordon on set at Carter's Unique Employment Agency in the 1972 season.

Below: Lucille Ball stars as Lucy Carter, Lucie Arnaz is her daughter Kim and Gale Gordon her stuffy brother-in-law Harry Mooney, who runs Carter's Unique Employment Agency, where Lucy also works.

The Lucy Show
(1 October 1962–16 September 1968) **CBS**

Here's Lucy
(23 September 1968–2 September 1974) **CBS**

After her divorce from Desi Arnaz, Lucille Ball returned to the air in *The Lucy Show* as Lucy Carmichael, a recently widowed bank secretary. The show also featured Vivian Vance (from *I Love Lucy*) as her friend Vivian Bagley, Jimmy Garrett as Lucy's son Jerry, Candy Moore as her daughter Chris, Ralph Hart as Vivian's son Sherman, Dick Martin as Lucy's friend Harry and Charles Lane as the cantankerous Mr Barnsdahl, Lucy's boss. By 1963, Gale Gordon replaced Lane as boss Theodore Mooney. In 1965, all the cast were replaced except for Lucy and Gordon. The new format saw Lucy as a bank secretary in San Francisco and joining the cast were Roy Roberts as bank president Harrison Cheever and Mary Jane Croft as Lucy's friend, Mary Jane Lewis.

In September 1968, *Here's Lucy* succeeded *The Lucy Show*, with some further changes. Lucy now was Lucille Carter, the secretary at Unique Employment Agency, run by her brother-in-law, Harrison Carter (played by Gale Gordon). Also involved with the show now were her real-life children, Lucie Arnaz as Kim and Desi Arnaz Jr. as her son Craig. Many guest stars also made appearances as Lucy continued to be popular with viewers, including Richard Burton and Elizabeth Taylor, Ginger Rogers, David Frost, Joe Namath and Ann-Margaret.

Right: It's Christmas and Lucille Ball and her usually antagonistic banker, Mr Mooney (Gale Gordon), stop feuding in *Lucy the Choirmaster*.

Below: Lucille Ball and guest star Dinah Shore cool their heels while stuck on a 'ski lift high in the Colorado Rockies'...a studio backdrop.

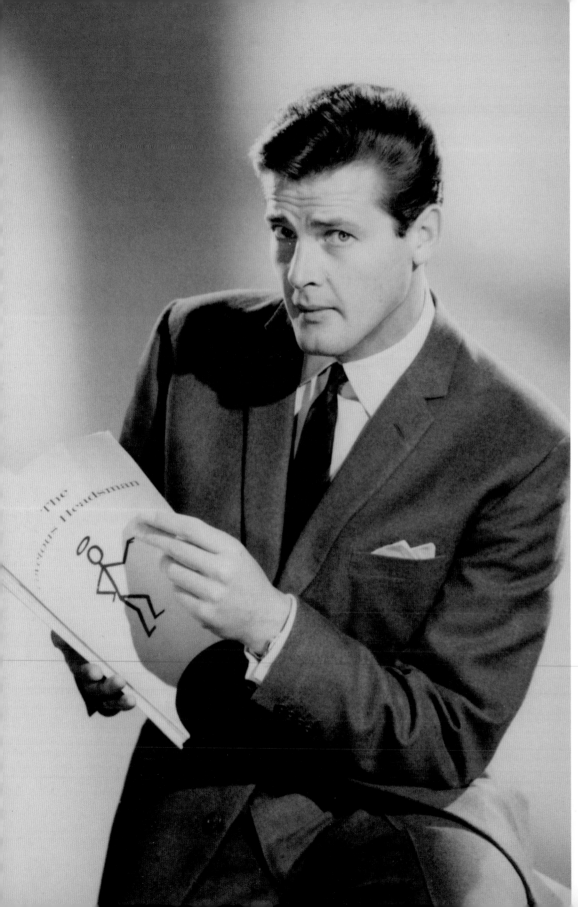

The Saint
(4 October 1962–9 February 1969)

The Saint starred Roger Moore (*left*) as Simon Templar, a suave and sophisticated investigator who mixed pleasure with business tracking down culprits, always with a beautiful woman not too far away. Based on the novels of Leslie Charteris, regulars included Winsley Pithey, Norman Pitt and Ivor Dean as Inspector Teal of Scotland Yard.

Did you know?

The TV show was so successful that the producers eventually ran out of books that were adaptable for TV scripts so they started sending Leslie Charteris ideas for new plotlines. He would give his opinions, ideas and (hopefully) his approval and those ideas would be made into scripts under his supervision. Remarkably, Charteris was also running out of ideas for stories for his *The Saint Magazine*. He was able to adapt the new TV scripts into new articles for the magazine.

The Saint on set in 1967, complete with fake background and all! (*Right*) Roger Moore, in his pre-James Bond role as Simon Templar: *The Saint*.

The Virginian
(19 September 1962–9 September 1970) NBC

The Virginian was the first 90-minute western series on television and starred James Drury as the mysterious Virginian, a taciturn foreman known simply as the Virginian, a man trying to come to grips with the inexorable westward advance of technology, culture and civilisation. A large cast included Lee J. Cobb as Judge Henry Garth, Doug McClure as Trampas, Gary Clarke as Steve, Pipa Scott as Molly Wood, Roberta Shore as Betsy, Randy Boone as Randy and Clu Gulager as Emmett Ryker. In the final season, the series was retitled *The Men from Shiloh*, with Stewart Grainger playing new owner Colonel Alan MacKenzie. James Drury and Doug McClure remained, and Lee Majors joined the show as hired hand Roy Tate.

Above: James Drury, *The Virginian*, on set in 1967

Near right: Lee J. Cobb played Judge Garth, a stern man respected by the townspeople and also a father figure to the Virginian.

Far right: Doug McClure with guest star Joan Collins in the 1967 episode 'The Lady from Wichita'.

Above: Lee Majors and James Drury in *The Virginian*.

Right: Leslie Nielsen (*right*) and
H. M. Wyant guest starred in the
1967 episode, 'The Fortress'.

General Hospital
(1 April 1963–17 September 2010) ABC

General Hospital was one of daytime television's biggest success stories. *General Hospital* aired its first episode on April Fools' Day in 1963. It ran for 30 minutes per episode until 1976 when it was expanded to 45 minutes and then to 60 minutes in 1978. John Berardino as Dr Steve Hardy, Emily McLaughlin as Nurse Jessie Brewer, Sharon DeBord plays a young nurse, among the cast celebrating the 2000th episode.

Right: John Beradino as Dr Steve Hardy and Roy Thinnes as Phil Brewer.

Going My Way

(3 October 1962–11 September 1963)
ABC

Gene Kelly took on Bing Crosby's Oscar-wining role as Father Chuck O'Malley, a light-hearted, progressive young priest assigned to a parish in a lower-class New York City neighbourhood. Crusty Parish Priest Father Fitzgibbon was played by Leo G. Carroll, while Dick York supported as Kelly's boyhood friend Tom Colwell.

Right: Gene Kelly as Father Charles O'Malley, his one and only attempt at a weekly television series.

Below: *Going My Way* with Gene Kelly on the cover of *TV Times*.

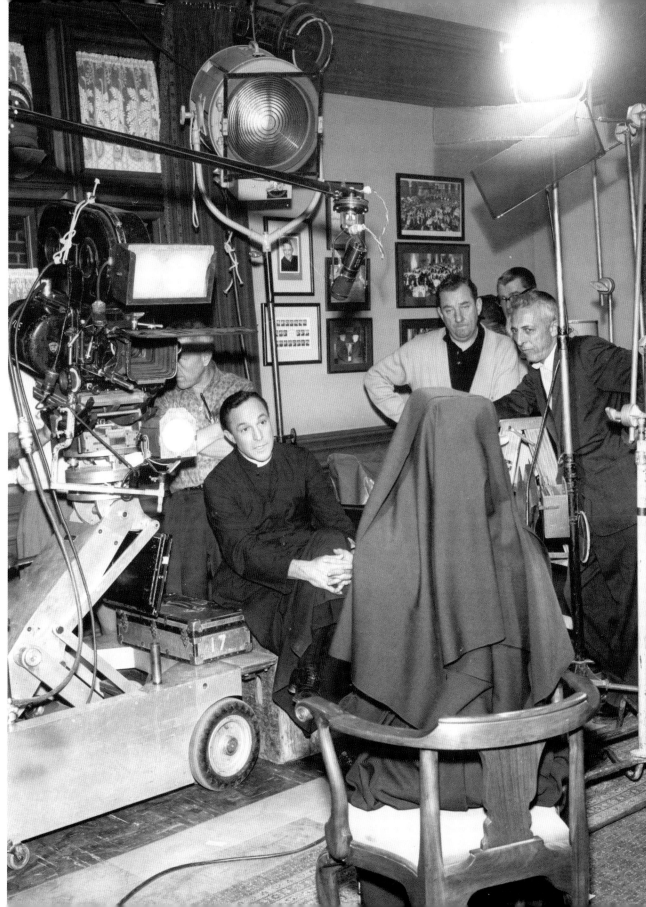

Laramie
(15 September 1959–17 September 1963) **NBC**

Two brothers, played by John Smith and Bobby Crawford Jr., determined to maintain the family ranch after the death of their father were the central characters of this western set in the Wyoming Territory of the 1870s. In addition to raising cattle, they used their ranch as a relay station for stagecoach traffic into and out of nearby Laramie. The Sherman brothers and a drifter, Jess Harper played by Robert Fuller, combine to run a stagecoach stop for the Great Central Overland Mail Company after the Sherman's father was murdered.

Left: John Smith as Slim Sherman and Robert Fuller as Jess Harper on *Laramie*.

Near right: John Smith, a veteran TV actor stars as Slim Sherman.

Far right: The stars of the show, including composer and actor Hoagy Charmichael (*far right*) on the cover of *TV Guide*.

160

Mister Ed

(1961) Syndicated,
(1 October 1961–4 September 1966) **CBS**

Mister Ed, a talking-horse didn't horse talk to everybody: in fact he would only talk to Wilbur Post (played by Alan Young). The confusion caused by a talking-horse, and the situations Ed got Wilbur into, an occasionally out of, formed the stories. In a rambling country home, Ed's stable was down the bottom of the yard, with Wilbur's work office (as an architect) nearby. The other cast included Connie Hines as Carol Post, Wilbur's wife (*left*), Larry Keating as their next door neighbour Roger Addison and Edna Skinner as Kay Addison his wife. The voice of Mister Ed was provided by Allan 'Rocky' Lane.

Did you know?

The palomino gelding Bamboo Harvester was made to move its lips to simulate 'talking' by rubbing peanut butter on its gums.

My Three Sons

(29 September 1960–2 September 1965), **ABC**
(16 September 1965–24 August 1972) **CBS**

Fred MacMurray stars as widower Steve Douglas, trying to raise three young boys (the eldest Mike played by Tim Considine, Robbie played by Don Grady and youngest Chip played by Stanley Livingstone), while William Frawley, the boy's grandfather 'Bub' O'Casey also lived with them and served as a housekeeper to the all-male clan. In the 1964–65 season, William Demarest took Frawley's place as their live-in 'Uncle Charley O'Casey'. Further changes were rung when Mike married and a 'new' son was adopted by the family. Mike, Robbie and Chip each got married on the show and in 1969 Steve Douglas finally remarried to Barbara Harper (played by Beverly Garland), who had a young daughter, Dodie.

Did you know?

Actor Fred MacMurray, the star of the show, filmed all his scenes across all the episodes in a season the opening weeks of production to free him up for film roles.

Left: The stars of the show (*from left to right*): Don Grady as Robbie Douglas, William Frawley as Francis 'Bub' O'Casey (*rear*) Stanley Livingston as Chip Douglas (*front*), Fred MacMurray as Steve Douglas (*seated*), Barry Livingston plays Ernie Thompson Douglas and let's not forget Tramp, the dog.

Right: A sad farewell in the 1966 season as Don Grady (*right*) decides to live away from home while attending college. Bidding him farewell are (*from left*) Fred MacMurray, William Demarest as Uncle Charley O'Casey, Barry Livingston and Stanley Livingston.

Above: Fred MacMurray and Don Grady (*rear*) with Stanley Livingston and William Demarest (*seated*) and Barry Livingston (*with his back to the camera*).

Right: Fred MacMurray listens to Stanley Livingstone's misunderstandings of the facts of life in 'Birds and Bees', the first episode of the 1961–62 season of *My Three Sons*.

Jackie Gleason

Left: Jackie Gleason....a larger than life character.

Below: On her 1967 show 'Movin' with Nancy,' Nancy Sinatra with her famous dad 'Old Blue Eyes,' Frank Sinatra.

Route 66

(7 October 1960–18 September 1964) **CBS**

Tod Stiles, played by Martin Milner, and Buzz Murdoch (George Maharis) were two young men who travelled around the country in Tod's Corvette in search of adventure.

Did you know?

Although the series was called *Route 66*, many of the episodes were set in areas in the United States that Route 66 did not travel through. The obvious choice for a *Route 66* theme song would have been the Bobby Troup song titled, *Get Your Kicks on Route 66* but CBS didn't care to pay royalties so they hired Nelson Riddle to write an instrumental theme for the series.

Right: Martin Milner who played Tod Stiles (*left*) and Glenn Corbett as Linc Case (*right*) with guest star Joan Crawford in the episode 'Same Picture, Different Frame'.

Below: *Route 66*, starring George Maharis (*left*) and Martin Milner on the cover of *TV Times*.

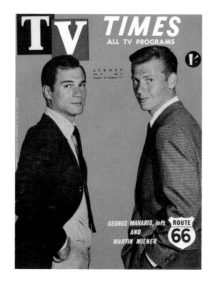

Did you know?

In real life, Wilfred Brambell was only 13 years older than Harry Corbett, but yet played his dad in the series. NBC made their own version of the series with Red Foxx titled *Sandford and Son* (1972–77).

Steptoe and Son

(1962–1965),
(1970–1974)

Steptoe and Son, the father and son rag-and-bone team, starring Wilfred Brambell (*left*) as the father, Albert, and Harry H. Corbett (*right*) as his son, Harold. Steptoe was a lazy, stubborn, narrow-minded old man. His son Harold was also obstinate, though prone to moments of enthusiasm and optimism, forever trying to move up in the world and escape from his dad. The episodes usually revolved around disagreements between the two men, Harold's efforts to better himself or his attempts to bed women. Harold's frustrations would see Albert nearly always come out on top, thwarting his son's attempts at every turn.

The Rag Trade
(6 October 1961–1963)

The Rag Trade was a comedy based in a small clothing workshop in London: Fenner Fashions. Reg Varney was brilliant as the foreman Reg and Miriam Karlin equally hilarious as shop steward Paddy Fleming. Peter Jones played Harold Fenner, who ran the workshop, with other cast members including Sheila Hancock as Carole, Barbara Windsor as Judy, Esma Reese Cannon as Lily Swann and Wanda Ventham as Shirley.

Stoney Burke

(1 October 1962–2 September 1963) **ABC**

Before *Hawaii Five-0* Jack Lord starred as *Stoney Burke,*
a rodeo performer, who was trying to become the world
champion saddle bronco rider and win the Golden Buckle.
Jack Lord plays Stoney Burke, a rodeo rider competing for
glory. The show follows his adventures with various people
and situations throughout the country.

Below: *Stoney Burke,* starring Jack Lord on the cover of *TV
Times* on 16 October 1963. The cast included Bruce Dern
as E. J. Stocker, Bill Hart as Red, Warren Oates as Ves
Painter and Robert Dowdell as Cody Bristol.

Combat

(2 October 1962–29 August 1967) **ABC**

Combat was the longest running of the several World War II dramas of the 1960s. Set in Europe, it told the story of one platoon and featured Rick Morrow as Sergeant Chip Saunders. The stories ranged from straight combat adventure to human interest and sometimes humorous themes, starting at the landing on D–Day.

Left: Vic Morrow starred as Sergeant 'Chip' Saunders in *Combat*, a World War II drama, based around his squad's battles against the Germans from the landing on D-Day as they fight their way through the French and Italian countryside.

Below: The crew gets ready to roll the cameras (and some duck for cover) as an explosion is detonated during filing in 1965. Rick Jason played Lieutenant Gil Hanley, Dick Peabody as Littlejohn, Pierre Jalbert as Cage, Steve Rogers and Conlan Cater as Doc, Jack Hogan as Kirby and Tom Lowell as Nelson

Above: *Combat* with Vic Morrow directing, in this two-part episode, 'Hells Are For Heroes'.

Near right: Rick Jason (*right*), real name Richard Jacobson, starred as Platoon Leader 2nd Lt. Gil Hanley in his most memorable television role. Also pictured is Pierre Jalbert (*left*) who played bilingual Cajun PFC Paul 'Caje' Le May. Jalbert was a junior and senior national ski champion, captaining the Canadian Olympic Ski Team at St Moritz, before a broken leg in practice robbed him of the chance to compete at the Games.

Did you know?

The contracts of Rick Jason and Vic Morrow guaranteed that each would receive equal top billing in Combat's opening credits. By the end of the series, each had been listed first 76 times. Lieutenant Hanley and Sergeant Saunders lost 118 men under their commands in combat during *Combat*'s run.

Above right: Shecky Greene learns about the privileges afforded rank from Keenan Wynn, guest starring as a bombastic cigar-chewing colonel.

The Gallant Men
(5 October 1962–14 September 1963) ABC

A World War II drama focusing on the American campaign in Italy, as seen through the eyes of a war correspondent, Conley Wright, played by Robert McQueeney. Other cast members included: Capt. Jim Benedict played by William Reynolds, Lt. Frank Kimro played by Robert Ridgely, PFC. Pete D'Angelo played by Eddie Fontaine, 1st Sgt. John McKenna played by Richard X Slattery. Private Ernie Lucavich played by Roland LaStarza, Private Sam Hanson played by Robert Gothie and Private Roger Gibson played by Roger Davis.

Left: The grim face of war….William Reynolds (*left*) and Robert McQueeney reflect the grimness of the battle ahead as they lead troops into a fight to save a convent filled with wounded soldiers in the episode, 'A Place to Die'.

Below: *The Gallant Men* (*left to right*): Anna Bruno-Lena plays Felicia, Victor Salinas is Pietro and Robert McQeeney is Conley Wright, in the episode 'Retreat to Concorde'. In this episode the squad is ordered to the town of Nieto for a mopping up operation before a German advance has them defending against the barrage.

The Man from UNCLE
(22 September 1964–15 January 1968) **NBC**

A light-hearted spy series which starred Robert Vaughn as Napoleon Solo and David McCallum as his partner in crime-fighting, Illya Kuryakin, with Leo G. Carroll as Alexander Waverly, head of UNCLE, which was an international crime-fighting organisation based in New York fighting the international crime syndicate THRUSH. The recurring theme each week had the agents requiring the help of an ordinary citizen to help save the world from THRUSH.

Did you know?

Robert Vaughn worked on his PhD during the course of the series, and often was allowed to leave the set early so that he could attend night classes. The success of the Man from UNCLE was so big by 1966 that it totally transformed the lives of its two stars. Vaughn has said that he actually became a recluse in his home because teenage girls would climb over his wall and hide in the bushes. David McCallum tried to go for a walk one day on Fifth Avenue in New York City and he was mauled so badly that police had to be called to rescue him.

Right: Robert Vaughn is Napoleon Solo in the hit spy-spoof series *The Man from UNCLE,* one of two agents (David McCallum as Illya Kuryakin) the series is centred around.

Below: David McCallum starred as the mysterious Russian agent Illya Kuryakin, who works for a fictitious secret international espionage and law enforcement agency named UNCLE.

Arrest and Trial

(15 September 1963–6 September 1964) **ABC**

Shown in two separate but interwoven 45-minute programmes the first section depicted the crime, the police investigation and the arrest. The second show depicted the trial. Chuck Connors (*left*) starred as public defender John Egan, Ben Gazzara (*right*) was Sergeant Nick Anderson, with John Larch as prosecutor Jerry Miller, Roger Perry as Detective Kirby and Noah Keen as Bone.

Did you know?

Ben Gazzara stood about 5'10" but Chuck Connors, was 6'6". Various 'tricks' were used to minimize the disparity in their sizes but sometimes filming the two standing together was unavoidable.

Near right: Anne Francis stars in the episode, 'The Witness': a teacher who can save an innocent boy from a murder charge, but who is afraid to testify on his behalf.

Far right: *Arrest and Trial* guest star, the beautiful Joey Heatherton. She proved a popular guest star in this era, appearing on many shows including *Mr Novak, The Virginian, What's My Line, The Tonight Show with Johnny Carson, The Andy Williams Show, The Hollywood Palace* and *The Ed Sullivan Show.*

Burke's Law
(20 September 1963–31 August 1965) **ABC**

Amos Burke Secret Agent
(15 September 1965–12 January 1966) **ABC**

Right: Gene Barry (*right*) starred as Amos Burke, a suave police chief of Los Angeles. A bachelor, he was independently wealthy and travelled around town in a chauffeured Rolls Royce. Also featured were Gary Conway as Detective Tim Tilson (*left*) and Regis Toomey as Detective Lester Hart. Most episodes were titled 'Who Killed...?' and featured cameo appearances by film stars such as Buster Keaton, Jayne Mansfield, Frank Sinatra and Terry Thomas to name a few. In 1965, the show's producers decided to make Burke a secret agent apparently to cash in on the success of NBC's 1964 smash *The Man from UNCLE*.

Did you know?

Burke's Law was Aaron Spelling's first big hit series. The first eight episodes of the show had 63 stars according to one ABC press release. Several of the Burke's Law writers, producers and others responsible for the show went on to create future series with a similar comedic-drama flare including *Columbo* (1971), *Murder She Wrote* (1984), *Matlock* (1986), and *Diagnosis Murder* (1993).

Below: The many faces of Carolyn Jones (who later starred as Morticia Addams of *Addams Family* fame) is Betsy Richards, Meredith Richards, Jane Richards and Olivia Manning in 'Who Killed Sweet Betsy'.

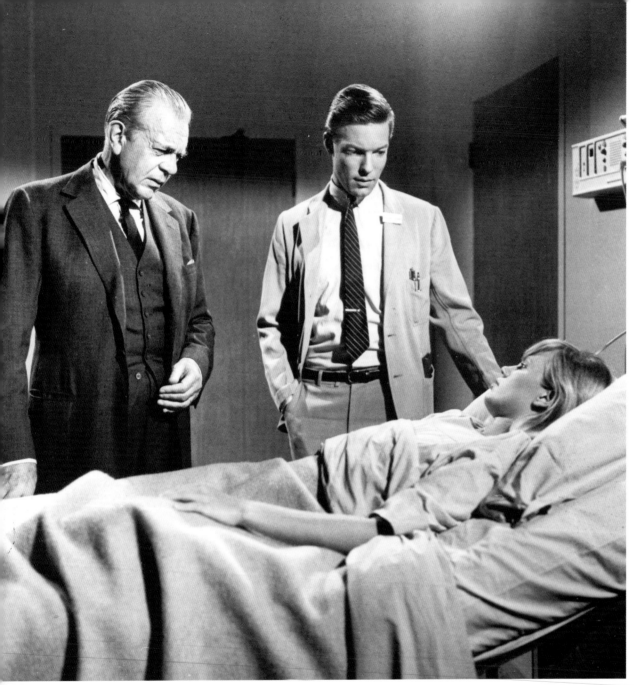

Dr Kildare
(28 September 1961–30 August 1966) **NBC**

In *Dr Kildare*, Richard Chamberlain (*centre*) starred as a serious, hard-working young intern, Dr James Kildare, working at Blair General Hospital. While trying to learn his profession, Kildare tried to also win the respect of senior specialist, Dr Leonard Gillespie, played by Raymond Massey (*left*). The popular series did not flinch from realistic situations of hospital life and the life-and-death aspect of the work.

Did you know?

The inspiration for the stories came from Dr George Winthrop Fish, a prominent urologist.

Right: *Dr Kildare*, with Dick Chamberlain and Raymond Massey on the cover of *TV Times*.

Flipper

(19 September 1964–2 September 1967) **NBC**

Right: The real star of the series was the dolphin, Flipper, who was both friend and helper in the weekly adventures of the Ricks family. The cast included Brian Kelly as Porter Ricks, chief ranger of Coral Key Park, Luke Halpin as Sandy Ricks, his 15-year-old son, and Tommy Norden as Bud Rix, his 10-year-old son. With their cottage situated on the shores of the park, the young boys more often than not got into danger, with Flipper regularly saving them.

Below: Actor Warren Day is sent flying from a punch by Porter Ricks (Brian Kelly) in the episode 'Flipper and the Fugitive'.

Gidget

(15 September 1965–1 September 1966) ABC

Sally Field made her television debut as Gidget, the 15½-year-old daughter of Professor Russ Lawrence, a widower. Gidget and her best friend Larue (Lynette Winter) managed to find endless fun in the sun of California.

Did you know?

Sally Field grew up in a 'show business' home. Her mother was popular 'B' movie actress Margaret Field. Her step-father was Jock Mahoney who has more than 90 acting credits and more than 60 credits as a stunt-double!

Left: The Gidget cast (*from left to right*): Gidget (Sally Field), her father Professor Russell Lawrence (Don Porter), older sister Anne Cooper (Betty Conner) and her TV husband John (Peter Deuel).

Right: Sally Field on the cover of *TV Guide* on 28 May 1966.`

Gomer Pyle, U.S.M.C.
(25 September 1964–19 September 1969) CBS

Right: *Gomer Pyle*, starred Jim Nabors, a good-natured Marine private whose naivety constantly had him at loggerheads with his drill instructor, Sergeant Carter played by Frank Sutton. The 'Pyle' character featured on the *Andy Griffith Show* but he gave up his job as a gas station attendant to join the Marine Corps, stationed at Camp Henderson, California.

Did you know?

Jim Nabors said that it was always difficult for him to watch the opening of the show because many of the men that he is seen marching with were killed in Vietnam. Although the series has a military setting, and the Vietnam War was raging at the time it originally aired, the war itself is never discussed.

Near right: Frank Sutton (*left*) as Sergeant Vince Carter, and Jim Nabors as Gomer Pyle.

Far right: In the episode, 'Corporal Carol,' with Corporal Carol Barnes (Burnett) putting the moves on Gomer endangering his relationship with his girlfriend Lou-Ann Poovie.

The Edie Adams Show: Here's Edie

(26 September 1963–19 March 1964) **ABC**

Starring Edie Adams, this was a variety/sketch comedy show also featuring Don Chastain, Peter Hanley and Dick Shawn. Some of the guests to appear on the show included: Zsa Zsa Gabor, Peter Falk, Bob Hope, Sid Caesar, Sammy Davis Jr., Bobby Darin, Johnny Mathis and Eddie Fisher.

Ernie Kovacs

(14 May 1951–24 August 1951, 4 January 1952–28 March 1952) **NBC**
(30 December 1952–14 April 1953) **CBS**
(12 December 1955–10 September 1956) **NBC**

Below: Husband and wife couple Edie Adams and Ernie Kovacs, who were married in September 1954, (seen here in August 1956). Sadly Ernie Kovacs died less than six years later from injuries sustained in a car accident in January 1962. Adams and Kovacs worked regularly together with talk-show pioneer, Jack Paar. In 1957, the two of them received Emmy nominations for best performances in a comedy series. Later, they played themselves in the final *Lucy-Desi Comedy Hour* television special. After Kovacs's death, Adams was given her own show, *Here's Edie*.

Above: *Here's Edie*. Edie Adams pulls the strings in a half-hour of musical fun and entertainment with a troupe of merry marionettes.

The Hathaways
(6 October 1961–30 March 1962) ABC

A situation comedy about a married couple who agree to take in a family of performing chimps Jack Weston (*left*) starred as real estate agent Walter Hathaway, with Peggy Cass (*right*) as his wife Eleanor. Also starring was Harvey Lembeck, as the chimps' agent, Jerry Roper, and the Marquis Chimps.

McHale's Navy
(11 October 1962–30 August 1966) **ABC**

Left: Ernest Borgnine (*left*) starred as Lieutenant Commander Quinton McHale, the commanding officer of the dysfunctional crew of PT-73 which is stationed at Taratupa in the Pacific Islands. The cast included Joe Flynn (*centre*) as Captain Wallace B. Binghamton, Tim Conway (*right*) as Ensign Charles Parker. Also featured were Carl Ballantine as Lester Gruber, George 'Christy' Christopher played by Gary Vinson, Harrison 'Tinker' Bell played by Billy Sands, Virgil Edwards played by Edson Stroll, Joseph 'Happy' Haines played by Gavin MacLeod, Fuji Kobiaji played by Yoshio Yoda and Lt. Elroy Carpenter played by Bob Hastings.

Below: The McHale's Navy crew aboard their PT-73 wish everyone a Happy Christmas in 1964.

Merry Christmas from all the gang

McHale's Navy SUNDAY 7.30 CHANNEL **9**

Right: Ernest Borgnine and Joe Flynn in character, with Captain Binghampton (*right*) looking concerned while McHale (*left*) looks decidedly relaxed by the situation.

Below: Claudine Longet who first appeared in the series in 'The Big Raffle', as Yvette Gerard, a French girl who Ensign Parker finds attractive. Jean Willes was Margot Monet, an owner of a gambling parlour in New Caledonia as well as McHale's old love interest.

Mr Novak

(24 September 1963–31 August 1965) **NBC**

James Franciscus starred as Mr John Novak, an English teacher at Jefferson High School in Los Angeles. Alongside Franciscus, Dean Jagger played principal Albert Vane, while Burgess Meredith succeeded Jagger for season two as principal Martin Woodbridge. The storyline followed the challengers of a young high school teacher on his first teaching job and his relationship with his older and experienced prinicipal, who while admiring the young man was not always in agreement with his methods.

Above: James Franciscus as Mr Novak, a first year English teacher at Jefferson High School, and Dean Jagger as Principal Albert Vane on set.

Right: James Franciscus with students on campus at Jefferson High School.

Petticoat Junction

(24 September 1963–12 September 1970) **CBS**

The small farming community of Hooterville provided the setting for this highly successful rural sitcom. Kate Bradley played by Bea Benaderet was the widowed owner of the Shady Rest Hotel. Helping her run the hotel were her three beautiful daughters: Bilie Jo played by Jeannine Ryley (later replaced by Gunilla Hutton and then Meredith MacRae), Bobbie Jo played by Pat Woodell (and then Lori Saunders) and Betty Jo played by Linda Kaye. Also assisting was the girls' Uncle Joe played by Edgar Buchanan. Kate's adversary was Homer Bedloe played by Charles Lane, the vice-president of the C. F. and W. Railroad, who was determined to close down the steam-driven branch of the railroad, affecting the good people of Hooterville (especially its two engineers, Charlie Pratt played by Smiley Burnette and Floyd Smoot played by Rufe Davis).

Did you know?

The dog on *Petticoat Junction* was never called by his name. They simply called him 'Dog'. In real-life, the dog's name was 'Higgins'. You might remember him better from his final acting role as the star of the 1974 movie, *Benji*. Ironically, that was also the final acting role for Edgar Buchanan who played Uncle Joe on *Petticoat Junction*!

Right: *Petticoat Junction* cast in front of the Shady Rest Hotel.

Peyton Place
(15 September 1964–2 June 1969) **ABC**

Based on Grace Metalious's best-selling novel, *Peyton Place* premiered with great expectations. The basic theme of the show involved the sexual going-ons of the lives of the residents of Peyton Place, a small New England town. The large cast included: Mia Farrow as Allison MacKenzie, Ryan O'Neal as Rodney Harrington, Dorothy Malone as Constance MacKenzie Carson, Tim O'Connor as Elliott Carson, Frank Ferguson as Eli Carson, Steven Oliver as Lee Webber, Chris Connelly as Norman Harrington, Barbara Parkins as Betty Anderson and Ed Nelson as Dr Michael Rossi.

Left: *Peyton Place* (*from left to right*), Mia Farrow plays Allison MacKenzie, the quiet but smart daughter of Constance, Ryan O'Neal is Rodney Harrington, the oldest son of Leslei and Catherine Harrington and Barbara Parkins is Betty Anderson, the daughter of George and Julie.

Below: Ed Nelson (*left*) as Dr Michael Rossi, the doctor who moved to Peyton Place from New York, while on the right is character actor Percy Rodriquez as Dr Harry Miles. The first episode opened with Rossi on the train heading towards Peyton Place and in the final scene after 514 episodes the show closes as he lies alone in a prison cell, facing trial for a crime of which he was innocent.

The Addams Family
(18 September 1964–2 September 1966) **ABC**

Right *The Addams Family* was a macabre, but always amusing, series, known as 'ghoul comedies' 'The Munsters'. Based on the comic strip drawn by Charles Addams, the cast of this short-lived but much-loved series included: Blossom Rock as Gomez's mother, Grandmamma, Carolyn Jones, Gomez's wife Morticia Addams, Lisa Loring as daughter Wednesday, Ted Cassidy as Lurch, the household's butler, John Astin as Gomez Addams, the head of the family, Jackie Coogan as Uncle Fester and Ken Weatherwax as their son Pugsley. Also featured in the series were Felix Silla as Cousin Itt and Ted Cassidy and director Jack Voglin, who would portray 'Thing', a disembodied hand that would appear out of a box.

Did you know?

As Gomez would often place his lit cigars into his pocket, the prop department had lined the pockets of John Astin's jackets with asbestos. And if Astin's characterisation of Gomez owes a lot to Groucho Marx, it might be because producer Nat Perrin was a former writer for the Marx Brothers in the 1930s and '40s.

It Takes a Thief
(9 January 1968–24 March 1970) **ABC**

Robert Wagner starred in this action-adventure series as Alexander Mundy, a professional thief who worked as a government agent in return for his release from prison. The series was inspired, but not a spin-off, of the classic Alfred Hitchcock movie 'To Catch a Thief' (1955) starring Cary Grant and Grace Kelly. Guest stars included such Hollywood stars as Fred Astaire Bette Davis, Joseph Cotten, Paul Henreid, Fernando Lamas and Ida Lupino.

Left: James Drury and Robert Wagner on set of It Takes a Thief in 1967.

Below: Robert Wagner and actress Sharon Acker on set in 1969.

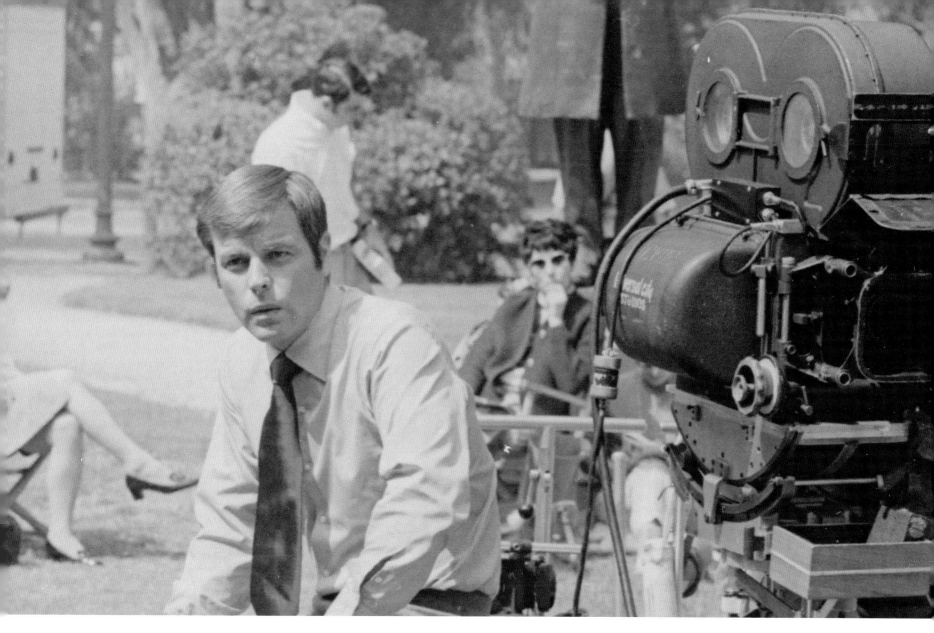

Above and right: Robert Wagner on the *It Takes a Thief* set. At the time, Wagner was divorced from wife Natalie Wood, but the pair reunited in the 1970s prior to her tragic death in a boating accident in November 1981.

The Beverly Hillbillies
(26 September 1962–7 September 1971) **CBS**

Left: Universally blasted by the critics on its premiere, *Hillbillies* climbed to the number-one spot by January 1964 and remained there through the year. It was the story of a backwards family who suddenly became rich when oil was discovered on their property. They immediately packed their belongings in their decrepit car and headed for California. (*Left to right, front seat*): Buddy Ebsen as J. D. 'Jed' Clampett, the head of the family and Max Baer Jr. as Jethro Bodine, while in the back seat are Donna Douglas as Elly May Clampett and Irene Ryan as Granny. Also in the show were: Raymond Bailey as Milburn Drysdale (their neighbour and president of Commerce Bank), Harriet E. MacGibbon as his wife Margaret and Nancy Kulp as Jane Hathaway, Drysdale's loyal and efficient secretary.

Below: Donna Douglas and Buddy Ebsen on the cover of *TV Times* on 7 August 1963.

Right: Irene Ryan, the matriarch of the family, was an angry short person with a short fuse to match. She would often be overruled by the calmer Jed.

Below: The Drysdales, Milburn and Margaret, in the foyer of the Clampett's Bevery Hills mansion.

The Big Valley
(15 September 1965–19 May 1969) **ABC**

The Big Valley told the story of the Barkleys, who lived on a 30,000-acre ranch in San Joaquin Valley, California. Barbara Stanwyck starred as widower and tough head of the family, Victoria Barkley, Richard Long played lawyer and calm eldest son, Jarrod, Peter Breck played number two son, an almost opposite to his elder brother, with a hot-headed personality. Lee Majors played Heath, the illegitimate half-Indian son of Victoria's late husband. Charles Briles played number four son Eugene and Linda Evans was beautiful daughter Audra.

Did you know?

The exterior of the Barkley's home on *The Big Valley* was also used as the Wilkes's Plantation exterior in the classic movie, *Gone with the Wind*.

Left: *The Big Valley*. Lee Majors stars as Heath Barkley and Linda Evans as Audra Barkley in the popular series.

Near right: Peter Breck is Nicholas 'Nick' Barkley, the hot-tempered younger son who managed the family ranch.

Far right: Barbara Stanwyck as Victoria Barkley, widow of Thomas and head of the wealthy, influential Barkley family. Stanwyck had a brilliant career as both a film and television star, appearing in 85 films (and being nominated for an Oscar for Best Actress on four occasions), before turning her acting skills to television, winning Emmy Awards for *The Barbara Stanwyck Show*, *The Big Valley* and *The Thorn Birds*.

190

Run for Your Life
(13 September 1965–27 March 1968) **NBC**

Run for Your Life was a drama series
starring Ben Gazzara (*right*) as a lawyer
Paul Bryan who only has a short time to
live. Bryan decides to travel and live his final
months to the fullest, with each episode
of the show featuring his encounters with
various people (played by top actors such as
Telly Savalas, Jack Albertson, Peter Graves,
Rita Moreno and Sal Mineo) in dramatic
situations. The series was created by
Roy Huggins, who had previously explored
a similar format with The Fugitive.
Interestingly, although Gazzara's character
was given no more than eighteen months to
live, the series ran for three seasons.

The Dean Martin Show
(The Dean Martin Comedy Hour)
(16 September 1965 – 24 May 1974) NBC

NBC almost begged Dean Martin to do a TV show because they were sure it would be a huge hit, but Dean was not particularly interested. He finally gave in when NBC agreed that he would not have to do any rehearsals and he would only have to show up one day per week on Sundays. Lee Hale would 'stand in' for Dean in one rehearsal on Saturday. NBC also agreed to pay Dean a salary greater than any other star at the time. Despite the demands, NBC came out fine as the show made big bucks! While popular guest stars were happy for the exposure they got on *The Dean Martin Show*, many of them did resent that they got no rehearsal with Dean. Dean would often make mistakes in his lines. Some guest stars just laughed it off when Dean would make some witty remark to the audience about how he was probably too drunk to remember his lines, or some other excuse. Some guest stars, however, didn't care much for the unprofessionalism. The audience loved it, though. The more mistakes Dean made, the louder they applauded and laughed.

Left: *The Dean Martin Show* was a runaway success story, astounding the entire television industry. Dean Martin is seen here on set in 1967.

Right: *The Dean Martin Show* Christmas holiday special won wide acclaim in 1967, with a medley of long-time favourites. Joining the Dean Martin family, (*from left to right, back row*): Ricci, Claudia, Deana, wife Jeannie and Craig. (*In front*): Gail, Dino, Gina and dad, were Frank Sinatra and his children, Nancy, Frank Jr. and Tina on a truly memorable night's entertainment.

Right: A cafe violinist, Sid Caesar invites
himself to the table of two patrons,
Dean Martin and Larri Thomas.

Below: You were always guaranteed a great
night's viewing when Dean Martin and Frank
Sinatra got together on stage or in front of a
camera, just like this occasion in 1969.

The Fugitive

(17 September 1963–29 August 1967) **ABC**

David Janssen was Richard Kimble, a physician who was falsely convicted of his wife's murder and sentenced to death. On the way to prison, under the care of Police Lieutenant Philip Gerard, he escapes after a train derailment. And so begins the search for the guilty one-armed man Kimble saw leaving the scene of the crime, while Gerard is equally determined to catch his escaped felon. When would the running stop?

Right: Barry Morse as the detective Philip Gerard, who will not stop until he has recaptured escaped felon Dr Richard Kimble.

Did you know?

Until the 'Who Shot J.R.?' episode of *Dallas* (1980), the finale of this series, where David Kimball finally catches the one-armed Man, was the highest-rated episode in the history of television. A record 72 percent of US homes tuned in to cheer David Kimble on in his quest.

Right: David Janssen has his hands full as he wrestles with a group of vigilantes in the episode 'Moon Child', in season two.

Below left: David Janssen, Jan Merlin and Arlene Martel star in 'The Blessings of Liberty', which aired on 23 November 1966.

Below right: David Janssen and Brenda Vaccaro, who played Joanne Spencer, in the episode, 'See Hollywood and Die'.

The Greatest Show on Earth
(17 September 1963–8 September 1964) **ABC**

Left: *The Greatest Show on Earth* was a drama about an American circus, starring Jack Palance as Johnny Slate the circus manager, produced by Desilu.

Below: Lucille Ball, who guest-starred as Kate Reynolds, together with Jack Palance in the episode, 'Lady in Limbo'.

The Dakotas

(7 January 1963–9 September 1963) **ABC**

Set in the Dakota Territory, a US Marshall and his deputies try and maintain law and order. Replacing *Cheyenne* it only had a short stint. Larry Ward starred as Marshall Frank Ragan, Chad Everett was Deputy Del Stark, Jack Elam was Deputy J. D. Smith (a former gunslinger) and Michael Green was deputy Vance Porter.

Right: Old Paint, a veteran performer of the silver screen in the 1960s. The 1000-pound horse was safely hoisted 30 feet up the sheer side of a cliff with the help of a special sling.

Below: *The Dakotas'* Jack Elam, a familiar, if not rugged, face on TV and film during the 1960s and 1970s.

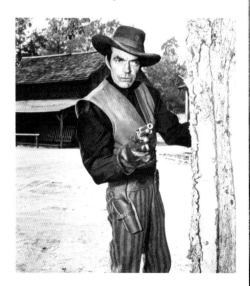

The Munsters
(24 September 1964–1 September 1966) **CBS**

The Munsters lived at 1313 Mockingbird Lane in Mockingbird Heights, in a cobweb-covered gothic mansion. While they considered themselves to be a normal American family, they looked to everyone else to be anything but normal (niece Marilyn aside). Fred Gwynne starred as Herman Munster, the 6'10" head of the family, who resembled Frankenstein's monster; Yvonne DeCarlo is his vamp-looking wife Lily; Beverly Owen (to December 1964) and Pat Priest (from January 1965) was their attractive niece, Marilyn; Al Lewis was Lily's 'very ancient' father, Grandpa and Butch Patrick was Edward Wolfgang (Eddie), Herman and Lily's young son.

Left: Fred Gwynne as Herman Munster, Yvonne De Carlo as his wife Lily. (*Left*) Beverley Owen who played Marilyn in episodes 1–13, while Pat Priest played her for episodes 14–70. (*Back left*) Al Lewis as Grandpa and (*back right*) Butch Patrick as Eddie Munster.

Above: *The Munsters* in one of their classic cars, which was designed by Tom Daniel and built by auto-customizer George Barris for the show.

Right: Fred Gwynne as Herman, the patriarch of the Munster household, who is employed by Gateman, Goodbury and Graves, a funeral home. His monstrous appearance was at odds with his good natured and childish behaviour.

Did you know?

Grandpa (played by Al Lewis, born in 1923) was one year younger than his daughter Lily (played by Yvonne De Carlo, born in 1922). Lewis and co-star Fred Gwynne had worked together on *Car 54 Where Are You?*

Voyage to the Bottom of the Sea

(14 September 1964–15 September 1968) **ABC**

An hour-long science fiction series created by Irwin Allen, who was also the executive producer, set aboard the *Seaview*, an American research atomic submarine with a glass nose, that roamed the seven seas, and whose crew came in contact with a never-ending parade of maniacs, monsters and aliens. The main cast included: Richard Basehart as Admiral Harriman Nelson, David Hedison as Captain Lee Crane, Bob Dowdell as Lt. Commander Chip Morton, Henry Kulky (1964–65) as CPO Curley Jones, Terry Becker (1965–68) as CPO Sharkey, Del Monroe as Kowalski and Paul Trinka as Patterson.

Above: David Hedison as Commander Lee Crane, who became the *Seaview*'s captain after the murder of her original commanding officer.

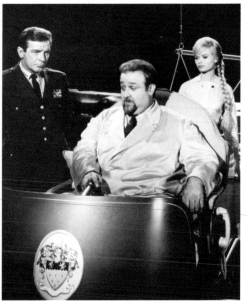

Right: Richard Basehart stars as Admiral Harriman Nelson, while Victor Buono and Brooke Bundy guest star in 'The Cybor' in season two. Oscar-nominated Buono (*What Ever Happened to Baby Jane*, 1962) was a regular guest star on many TV series during this time, including: *77 Sunset Strip*, *The Untouchables*, *The Wild Wild West*, *Perry Mason*, *Batman*, *Get Smart*, *Hawaii Five-0* and *The Odd Couple*.

200

Days of Our Lives
(8 November 1965–) **NBC**

Macdonald Carey, best known for his role as the patriarch Dr Tom Horton in the long-running soap *Days of our lives* is seen here in an earlier role. Carey had been a successful radio actor and stage performer before starting a film career in the early 1940s (*The Great Gatsby*, 1949). He also enjoyed many appearances on various series, including *Wagon Train*, *Mr Novak* and *The Outer limits*.

Did you know?

After Frances Reid passed away in February 2010, Susan Seaforth Hayes became the only remaining cast member who has appearing on the series since its premiere. She is also the only cast member to appear during all six decades *Days of Our Lives* has been on air.

Below: Macdonald Carey with Susan Flannery and Susan Seaforth on the cover of *TV Times* on 1 March 1975.

The Patty Duke Show

(18 September 1963–31 August 1966) **ABC**

The Patty Duke Show was a situation comedy starring the very talented teenager Patty Duke, who had won the Academy Award for Best Supporting Actress (for *The Miracle Worker*) the previous year. Patty played identical cousins, Patty and Cathy Lane. Patty was a typical, outgoing American teenager, while cousin Cathy, who was living with Patty's family while her father was overseas, was a more reserved and studious English teenager. Between the two of them they confused family, friends and neighbours alike by trading places as identical twins, with no one able to tell them apart. The supporting cast included William Schallert as Patty's father, Martin Lane; Jean Byron as Patty's mother, Natalie Lane; Paul O'Keefe as Patty's younger brother, Ross and Eddie Applegate as Richard Harrison, Patty's boyfriend.

Left: Patty Duke stars as Patty Lane, a 'normal' teenager living with her family in her family home in Brooklyn Heights.

Below: The entire cast of the show in the living room of the family home, including Patty Dukes' 'double' standing in for the character of Cathy.

Did you know?

Patty Duke was so convincing playing both parts that fans wrote to the show's producers asking who the actress was that played cousin Cathy

Right: Paul O'Keefe asks his 'sister' Patty Duke to help him find a way to get on the Little League Baseball team in the episode 'Take Me Out To the Ball Game'.!

Right: The many faces of Patty Duke in character

Family Affair
(12 September 1966–9 September 1971) **CBS**

Left: This saccharin-sweet sitcom was saved by the cuteness of its two child co-stars, Anissa Jones as Buffy and Johnny Whitaker as her twin Jody. It starred Brian Keith as bachelor Bill Davis, who suddenly found himself responsible for his nephew and two nieces. Despite initial misgivings, Bill and French became very attached to the children and learned to adjust their lifestyle to make room for them. Pictured are Kathy Garver (Cissy), Anissa Jones (Buffy), (second row) Johnny Whitaker (Jody), Brian Keith (Bill Davis) and (top) Sebastian Cabot (Mr French).

Below: Johnnie Whitaker, Brian Keith and Anissa Jones on the cover of TV Times on 14 May 1969.

Above: *A Family Affair's* young cast, (*from left*) Anissa Jones, Kathy Garver and Johnny Whitaker.

Right: Veterans Brian Keith (*left*) and Sebastian Cabot (*right*) with the young cast of *A Family Affair*. While the show proved to be the biggest hit of character actor Brian Keith's career, Sebastian Cabot didn't really care for the role as Giles French when he read the script for the pilot. He felt that the stiff upper-lipped English butler would be a boring part to play. He agreed to do the pilot only because the money was very good.

Did you know?

In the episode that Buffy broke her leg, Anissa Jones had really broken her leg and the writers came up with the script for that episode in one day. Although the Buffy character was six years old, Anissa was already 8 when the series began and just one week short of 13 when the last episode aired. As she got older, the show's producers ordered Anissa to bind her chest tightly, dress younger and carry her famed Mrs Beasley doll in as many scenes as possible. Jones tragically died of a drugs overdose in 1976, aged 18.

Left: Batman and Robin in their helicopter, tackling crime.

Below: Adam West (Bruce Wayne) gives Burgess Meredith (The Penguin) something to think about, 1966.

Batman

(12 January 1966–14 March 1968) **ABC**

Adam West, who had been featured on *The Detectives*, was Bruce Wayne, a Gotham City millionaire whose secret identity was Batman, a masked, caped crusader who used sophisticated paraphernalia to capture crooks. His sidekick was Robin, who played Dick Grayson (the Boy Wonder), real name Burt Ward. Together, the Dynamic Duo helped the usually impotent police force to keep Gotham City's streets a safe place. Alan Napier played Alfred Pennyworth, Wayne's butler, Madge Blake was Dick's aunt Harriet Cooper, Neil Hamilton was Police Commissioner Gordon and Stafford Repp was Chief O'Hara. Among a host of guest villains were Burgess Meredith as The Penguin, Frank Gorshin as The Riddler, Eartha Kitt as Catwoman, George Sanders as Mr Freeze, Cesar Romero as The Joker, Vincent Price as Egghead, Milton Berle as Louie The Lilac, Tallulah Bankhead as The Black Widow and Ethel Merman as Lola Lasagne. During the numerous fight scenes, the words 'POW!', 'BANG!', 'THUD!' and others would appear on the screen. That was a reflection of what happened in the Batman comic books

Right Frank Gorshin was brilliant as The Riddler, guest-starring in the opening two-part episode, 'Hi Diddle Riddle' and 'Smack in the Middle'.

Did you know?

One of the guest villains on the show, Pierre Salinger, who played Lucky Pierre, was the former press secretary to President John Kennedy. The only character ever killed off on the show was Molly, one of The Riddler's hench-people, who was played by Jill St John. Alan Napier, who was excellent as the Batman's English butler, in real life had a very famous cousin named Neville Chamberlain, who just happened to be the British Prime Minister from 1937–1940.

Near right: Batman and Batgirl, played by Yvonne Craig. As Commissioner Gordon's daughter, Barbara Gordon, a librarian, appeared in the final 1967–68 season.

Far right: Cesar Romero played the role of The Joker from 1966 to 1968. He refused to shave his moustache for the role, so white face makeup was smeared over it.

Bewitched

(17 September 1964– 1 July 1972) **ABC**

An enchanting witch Samantha Stevens, played by Elizabeth Montgomery, was married to a mere mortal, Darren (Dick York, 1964–69, and Dick Sargent,1969–72). Samantha's meddlesome mother Endora was played by Agnes Moorehead. David White was Larry Tate, Darren's boss in a New York advertising agency. Samantha's trademark was to twitch her nose to make magic happen.

Above: Three very popular and talented actresses of the era on the set of *Bewitched*, Elizabeth Montgomery, Marlo Thomas and Judy Carne.

Right: Elizabeth Montgomery, Dick York and Tabatha of *Bewitched* on the cover of *TV Times* on 19 April 1967.

Left: Dick York and Cheryl Holdridge in the episode 'The Girl Reporter'. A talented actor, York was forced to surrender the role in 1969 because of chronic back trouble.

Below: Elizabeth Montgomery and Agnes Moorehead on the cover of TV Times.

The Bing Crosby and Bob Hope Chrysler Special

(4 October 1963–6 September 1967) **NBC**

Film and radio favourites Bob Hope (*left*) and Bing Crosby (*right*) also found a home on television with a number of 'specials' produced during the 1950s, 1960s and 1970s, right up to Crosby's death in 1977. The pair had starred in a number of successful 'Road to …' comedies and their banter and musical talent easily transferred to the small screen.

Left and below: Bing and Bob live on air.

Right: Bing is joined by guests
Frank Sinatra and Dean Martin in 1964.

Below: *The Bing Crosby and Bob Hope
Chrysler Special*, 1965.

Daktari

(11 January 1966–15 January 1969) **CBS**

An African adventure series set at the Wameru Study Centre for Animal Behaviour, on Daktari the animals, Clarence the cross-eyed lion and Judy the chimp were as popular as its human stars. The *Daktari* cast was Cheryl Miller as Paula Tracy, Marshall Thompson as Dr Marsh Tracy, Yale Summers as Jack Dane and Clarence the cross-eyed lion.

Right: Cheryl Miller, daughter of Dr Tracy, with Judy the chimpanzee in 1967.

Did you know?

Daktari means 'doctor' or 'healer' in Swahili.

Daniel Boone

(24 September 1964–27 August 1970) **NBC**

Based loosely on the life of the American pioneer who was instrumental in the settlement of Kentucky during the 1770s, Fess Parker starred as Daniel Boone. Also featured were Ed Ames as Mingo, Boone's friend and college-educated Cherokee, Pat Blair as Rebecca Boone (Daniel's wife), Darby Hinton as Israel and Veronica Cartwright as daughter Jemima. A decade earlier, Fess Parker had skyrocketed to stardom as Walt Disney's Davy Crockett, another American folk hero.

Right: Fess Parker and Ezekial Williams in 'The Far Side of Fury'.

Below: *Daniel Boone* stars Fess Parker, Darby Hinton and Patricia Blair on the cover of *TV Guide*.

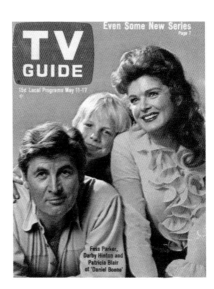

The Dick Van Dyke Show

(3 October 1961–7 September 1966) **CBS**

A classic comedy, it was one of the first series in which the central characters worked for a television series. Dick Van Dyke starred as Rob Petri, Mary Tyler Moore was his wife Laura, Larry Matthews was their son Richie, Morey Amsterdam was Buddy Sorrell, Rose Marie was Sally Rogers, Richard Deacon was Mel Cooley and Carl Reiner was Alan Brady. The show centred around a mythical comedy show, *The Alan Brady Show*, for which Rob Petrie was the head comedy writer. Working with Rob were two other writers, Sally and Buddy. Their nemesis at the office was Mel Cooley, the pompous producer. Episodes focused on Rob and Laura's home life as well as the problems of the writers.

Left and below: The stars of the show, Mary Tyler Moore and Dick Van Dyke, who play husband and wife pair Rob and Laura.

Did you know?

Carl Reiner played the role of Rob Petrie in the series' pilot. We all know that Dick Van Dyke was chosen for the part on the series but what is little known is that Johnny Carson was the second choice for the role. The role of Laura Petrie was a little harder to cast. More than 60 actresses were auditioned before Mary Tyler Moore was selected. Mary's first on-screen appearance was as Happy Hotpoint, an elf in the Hotpoint appliance commercials that appeared on the *Adventures of Ozzie and Harriet* (1952).

Right: Dick Van Dyke and Morey Amsterdam in a 1965 episode.

Below: Rob and Laura try unsuccessfully to spark a romance with Sally and Laura's cousin in the 1961 episode, 'Sally and the Lab Technician'.

Dragnet

(16 December 1951–6 September 1959),
(12 January 1967–10 September 1970) **NBC**

Dragnet was one of the most famous crime shows in television history. It starred Jack Webb (*below*) as Sergeant Joe Friday, a hard-working Los Angeles cop who seemed to have no personal life and no interest other than police work. Barney Phillips was originally Friday's partner Sergeant Ed Jacobs, before Harry Morgan joined when the show returned in the 1960s.

Left: Harry Morgan and Jack Webb star as police detectives Officer Bill Gannon and Sgt. Joe Friday in *Dragnet*.

Did you know?

The number 714 was selected to be Friday's badge number as a way to pay homage to Babe Ruth's all-time home run record, which at the time was 714. Jack Webb was the creator, star, and executive producer of *Dragnet*. His main concern was that the show would follow the real-life daily duties of police detectives. He insisted that the step-by-step work involved in an investigation and arrest be accurately shown. George Fenneman (Groucho Marx's sidekick in *You Bet Your Life*, 1950) read the opening narrative on this series and the radio version of *Dragnet*. Hal Gibney subsequently read it for the 1967–1970 series.

Garrison's Gorillas
(5 September 1967–17 September 1968) **ABC**

This World War II drama was inspired by the film *The Dirty Dozen*. It starred Ron Harper as Lieutenant Craig Garrison, an army officer who put together a squad of four men, all of whom were serving time in federal prison. The men were promised pardons in exchange for their co-operation. It starred Chris Cary as Goniff, a pickpocket, Rudy Solari as Casino, a thief, Brendon Boone as Chief, a knife-wielding Indian and Cesare Danova, as Actor, a conman. Together, they use their special skills against the Germans in WWII.

Top: Martine Collette who played Marie in the debut season episode in 1967.

Bottom: Brendon Boone in a street battle in 1967.

Green Acres

(15 September 1965–7 September 1971) **CBS**

Oliver Wendell Douglas (played by Eddie Albert) was a highly successful Manhattan lawyer who longed to get closer to nature. Ignoring the objections of his socialite wife Lisa (played by Eva Gabor), Oliver bought a 160-acre farm just outside the town of Hooterville, sight-unseen from My Haney (played by Pat Buttram), a fast-talking local who tried to sell the couple everything. The cast of the show (*back row from left to right*): Alvy Moore (county agent Hank Kimball), Tom Lester (glib farmhand Eb Dawson), Pat Buttram (slimy salesman Mr Haney). (*Front row*) Eva Gabor (Oliver's wife Lisa Douglas), Eddie Albert (Oliver Wendell Douglas) and Eleanor Audley (Oliver's mother).

Right: The zany but loveable Eva Gabor with Eddie Albert.

Below: Robert Culp and Bill Cosby on the cover of *TV Guide* on 25 March 1967.

I Spy
(15 September 1965–2 September 1968) **NBC**

I Spy was the story of two fun-loving undercover agents (both graduates) who travelled the world on assignments, starring Robert Culp as Kelly Robinson, who masqueraded as a tennis pro travelling around the world in tournaments, and Bill Cosby as Alexander Scott, his trainer. Culp and Cosby improvised most of their banter and rewrote much of their dialogue as they were often dissatisfied with the scripts. *I Spy* was the first TV show to have an African-American star cast in a lead role.

Above: Bill Cosby and Leslie Uggams on location in Italy in 1967.

219

Lost In Space
(15 September 1965–11 September 1968) **CBS**

Set in 1997, the story traces the adventures of the 'Space' Family Robinson, after their spaceship was sabotaged and thrown hopelessly off course by stowaway Dr Zachary Smith (played by Jonathan Harris). The spaceship's mission had been to take the Robinson family on a five-year voyage to a planet in the Alpha Centauri solar system. Instead they were stranded on an unknown planet and forced to deal with monsters, aliens and any number of setbacks, with Smith usually at the centre of most of their troubles. Guy Williams played Professor John Robinson, June Lockhart was his wife Maureen, Mark Goddard played Don West, the pilot, Marta Kristen was eldest daughter Judy Robinson, Billy Mummy was young son Will, Angela Cartwright was youngest daughter Penny, Bob May played the robot and Dick Tufeld provided the robot's voice.

Did you know?

In order to keep their budgets as low as possible, it was common to share props from one program to another. Some of the props, including the robot in *Lost in Space* were also used on *Voyage to the Bottom of the Sea* (1964), *Batman* (1966), *Time Tunnel* (1966), and *Land of the Giants* (1968).

Left: Jonathan Harris who played Dr Zachary Smith with The Robot (voice played by Dick Tufeld. Harris's character was unique in that he provided both the menace and the comedy in *Lost in Space*, and he manipulated the robot and befriended Wil (Billy Mumy) to get his way. Many of his sayings ('Never Fear, Smith is here!' and 'You bubble-headed booby!') gave him a cult following around the world.

Near Right: Guy Williams as Dr John Robinson, astrophysicist and head of the mission and father.

Far Right: The 'Space Family Robinson' (*from left*): June Lockhart, Guy Williams, Marta Kristen, Mark Goddard, Billy Mummy, Jonathan Harris and Angela Cartwright

Mission Impossible

(17 September 1966–8 September 1973) **CBS**

The basis for this series was the top-secret assignments taken on by this elite group of agents, usually involving disrupting the activities of various small foreign powers seeking to create problems for America or the free world. All the plans executed by the Impossible Missions Force were incredibly complex and depended on split-second timing and an astounding feat of sophisticated electronic gadgetry. The leader of the group (Jim Phelps played by Peter Graves), devised the complex plans used to accomplish the team's missions. Barney Collier played by Greg Morris, was the electronics expert and Willie Armitage played by Peter Lupis provided muscle throughout the series run. Rollin Hand played by Martin Landau was an expert at disguise and Cinnamon Carter played by Barbara Bain was the versatile, beautiful, female member of the team.

Left: (*Left to right*): (*top*) Peter Graves and Lynda Day George, (*bottom*) Greg Morris and Peter Lupus.

Below: The agents on the cover of *TV Guide* on 8 February 1969.

Did you know?

Nearly every non-lead actor or actress that worked on *Star Trek* also appeared in *Mission Impossible*. Lead *Star Trek* performers who guest-starred include George Takei, William Shatner, and eventual series regular Leonard Nimoy. The *Mission Impossible* TV show was so popular that it attracted some of the biggest guest stars of the time…Elizabeth Ashley, Ed Asner (*Lou Grant*), Tom Bosley (*Happy Days*), Lloyd Bridges (*Sea Hunt*), Jack Cassidy, Joan Collins, Robert Conrad (*Baa Baa Black Sheep*), Tyne Daly (*Judging Amy*), Will Geer (*The Waltons*), Robert Goulet, Fernando Lamas, Larry Linville (*MASH*), Roddy McDowall (*Planet of the Apes*), Darren McGavin, Lee Meriwether (*Time Tunnel*), Sal Mineo, Ricardo Montalban (*Fantasy Island*), Vic Morrow (*Combat*), Pernell Roberts (*Bonanza*), William Shatner (*Star Trek*), Martin Sheen (*The West Wing*), Dean Stockwell (*Quantum Leap*), Loretta Swit (*MASH*), and Ray Walston (*My Favorite Martian*).

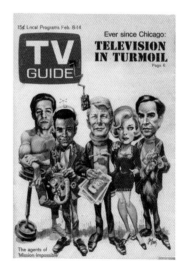

Star Trek

(8 September 1966–2 September 1969) **NBC**

One of the few series to prove more popular in syndication than in its three-year network run, *Star Trek* acquired a fiercely loyal cult following. Set in the 22nd century aboard the starship *Enterprise*, *Star Trek*'s voyagers were commissioned to embark on a five-year mission to 'seek out new life and new civilisations'. The series highlighted differences between mankind and other life forms, ranging from gaseous beings to species similar to humanoids. The main cast comprised of: William Shatner as Captain James Kirk, Leonard Nimoy as Science Officer Spock, DeForest Kelley as medical officer Dr Leonard 'Bones' McCoy, James Doohan as chief engineer Montgomery Scott ('Scotty'), Michelle Nichols as communications officer Lieutenant Uhara, George Takei as navigator Mr Sulu, Majel Barrett as chief nurse Christine Chapel and Walter Koenig as navigator Ensign Chekov.

Did you know?

In the hallways of the *Enterprise* there are tubes marked 'GNDN'. These initials stand for 'goes nowhere does nothing'.

Right: (*left to right*): Mr Sulu, Lt Uhura, Ensign Chekov, Dr Leonard Bones McCoy.

Opposite: *Star Trek* Captain James T. Kirk and Mr Spock.

That Girl

(8 September 1966–10 September 1971) **ABC**

That Girl was a prototype for a wave of 'independent women' series. Marlo Thomas played Ann Marie, a high-spirited young actress who had left the comfort of her parents' home to build a career in New York. To support her fledging acting career she took on odd jobs in offices and department stores. She met Don Hollinger (played by Ted Bessell) who became her first romance.

Left: Marlo Thomas and Ted Bessell.

Did you know?

Marlo Thomas is married to talk-show personality Phil Donahue. She is the daughter of Danny Thomas, who previously starred in his show, *Make Room for Daddy* (1953). Her father also guest-starred on *That Girl* in episode #127, 'Those Friars'.

The Bob Newhart Show
1961

Bob Newhart (*above*) was part of the new wave of comedians in the 1960s. A former copyrighter for an advertising agency, Newhart's understated, stammering and sardonic delivery was best shown on Christmas Specials and guest appearance in the 1960s before he starred in two highly successful sitcom formats–the first in 'The Bob Newhart Show' from 1972 to 1978, and secondly in 'Newhart' from 1982 to 1990.

Right: Bob Newhart on the phone on set of *The Bob Newhart Show* in 1961.

The Hollywood Palace

(4 January 1964–7 February 1970) **ABC**

The Hollywood Palace was a lavish, big-budget, big-name variety show. A different host topped the bill each week, such as: Bing Crosby, Fred Astaire, Milton Berle, Jimmy Durante, Maurice Chevalier, Gene Barry, Tony Randall, Don Adams, Sid Caesar and Sammy Davis Jr., to name just a few.

Left: *The Hollywood Palace* host Milton Berle.

Below right: Host for the night, Maurice Chevalier.

Below left: Joe Flynn, Ernest Borgnine and Carl Ballantine of McHale's Navy fame on the variety show *The Hollywood Palace*.

Right: Cyd Charisse and husband
Tony Martin in 1964.

Below: Tony Randall and Vikki Carr.

Danger Man

(1960–1962 and 1964–1968) UK

Patrick McGoohan starred as secret agent John Drake in this series financed by Lew Grade's ITC Entertainment. Danger Man was known as *Secret Agent* in the United States, and *Destination Danger* and *John Drake* in other parts of the world.

Opposite: Judy Garland (*right*) and Vic Damone on *The Hollywood Palace*, 1964.

The Guns of Will Sonnett
(8 September 1968–15 September 1969) ABC

A grizzled, old, ex-cavalry scout, Will Sonnett, played by Walter Brennan, and his grandson, played by Dack Rambo, searched the west for the boy's father in this unusual western set in the 1870s. The final episode of the *Guns of Will Sonnett* was broadcast six months after the previous episode. The series had been cancelled without story-lines being resolved. In an unusual move, ABC filmed a 'wrap-up' episode that made fans very happy. With all three family members reunited, grandpa took a job as the sheriff of an old western town, and his son and grandson became his deputies.

Left: Dack Rambo.

Below: Walter Brennan and Dack Rambo.

Walter Brennan
Dack Rambo
GUNS OF
WILL SONNETT

The Monkees

(12 September 1966–19 August 1968) **NBC**

Inspired by the success of The Beatles' movies, *A Hardy Day's Night* and *Help*, open auditions were held at NBC, which resulted in over 400 actors being tested by producers Bert Schneider and Robert Rafelson. Eventually, four young men, actors Micky Dolenz and Davy Jones and musicians Mike Nesmeth and Peter Tork, formed The Monkees. The show was a mixture of comedy one-liners and fast and slow motion comic routines, with The Monkees singing their hit songs, which were written by the best young talent available: *Last Train to Clarkesville* (Boyce and Hart), *I'm a Believer* (Neil Diamond) and *Take a Giant Step* (Goffin and King). The group would break up shortly after the series finished in 1968, but not before taking control of their music (they were not allowed to play on their early records) and touring the world as a real rock and roll band.

Right: (*left to right*) Mike Nesmeth, Micky Dolenz (*and in front*) David Jones, Peter Tork.

Below: The Monkees rivalled The Beatles for popularity and record sales for a brief time in 1966–1967.

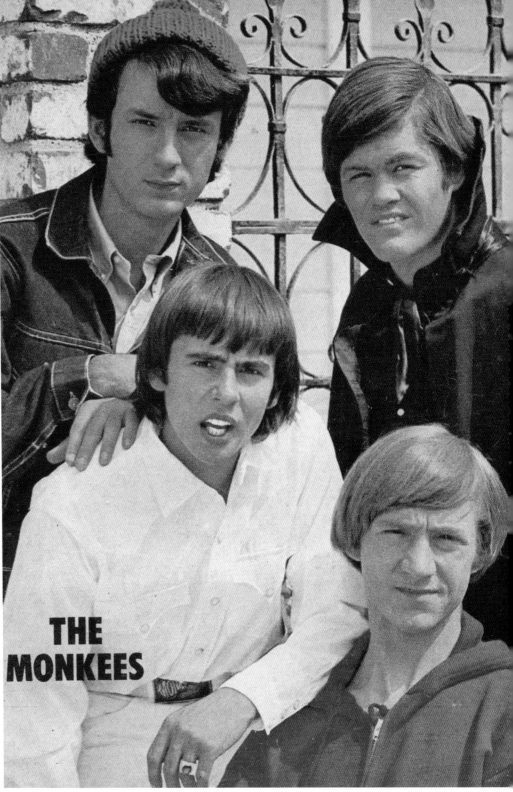

The Wild, Wild West
(17 September 1965–19 September 1969) CBS

A fantasy western starring Robert Conrad (*right*) as James West, a special agent assigned to the frontier by President Ulysses S. Grant. His associate and co-star was Ross Martin, who played Artemus Gordon (*left*). The pair battled an assortment of mad scientists and crazed outlaws, travelling in a special railroad car that supplied them with the materials to concoct all manner of bizarre weapons and devices to foil their adversaries. Also appearing were Michael Dunn as Dr Miguelito Loveless, West's diminutive arch-enemy, James Gregory as President Grant and Charles Aidman as Jeremy, who joined the show when Ross Martin suffered a mild heart attack.

Did you know?

Robert Conrad (5'8") wore 3" heels as Jim West and the CBS casting office had orders not to hire any women over 5'6" for the show.

Laugh-In
(22 January 1968–14 May 1973) NBC

Hosted by comedy duo Dan Rowan (*left*) and Dick Martin, *Laugh-In* was a fast-moving hour of gags, one-liners and short pieces that proved an immediate hit with a cast of brilliant performers. With the famous line, 'Sock it to me', uttered on many occasions and with regular 'nuts' of the calibre of: Chelsea Brown, Ruth Buzzi, Judy Carne, Henry Gibson, Goldie Hawn, Dennis Allen and Johnny Brown to mention just a few, many gags were crammed into the one hour timeslot, making it a huge success. The show will also be remembered for the closing lines of the compares, 'Goodnight Dick and goodnight Dick'.

Did you know?

Many movie celebrities and politicians made cameo appearances on Rowan and Martin's *Laugh In*. In 1968, in the lead-up to the US Presidential race, Richard Nixon appeared on the show, voicing the well-known phrase, 'Sock It to Me'. Hubert Humphrey, who was running against Nixon, was also invited to appear but declined.

Below: The Little Old Man (Arte Johnson) and bride-to-be Gladys Ormphby (Ruth Buzzi).

Gilligan's Island

(26 September 1964–4 September 1967) **CBS**

The small charter boat *Minnow* had been on a sightseeing party when it was caught in a storm and wrecked on the shore of an unchartered South Pacific island. Marooned together on the island were Gilligan, played by Bob Denver, the good-natured skipper, played by Alan Hale, a millionaire and his wife played by Jim Backus and Natalie Schafer, a sexy movie star played by Tina Louise, a high-school science professor played by Russell Johnson, and a naive country girl played by Dawn Wells. 109a: The full cast flank creator Sherwood Schwartz and director Jack Arnold.

Above: The cast of *Gilligan's Island*, described by one critic as 'The most inane sitcom ever conceived'. The passengers were never actually rescued before the series ended in 1967, although the situation was later resolved with a series of reunion specials in the 1970s and 1980s

Did you know?

In the very first shot of the opening credits, the American flag over the harbor can be seen flying at half-mast. The reason was that the assassination of President John F. Kennedy occurred shortly before the shot was filmed.

Right: Gilligan with gorilla. Denver's character was not that far removed from his Maynard G. Krebs character from *The Many Loves of Dobie Gillis*.

235

I Dream Of Jeannie

(18 September 1965–1 September 1970) **NBC**

Astronaut Tony Nelson (played by Larry Hagman) was on an aborted space mission that forced him to parachute onto a desert island. There, he found an old bottle that had apparently washed ashore. Opening the bottle, out popped a 2000-year-old genie who promptly accepted him as her master since he had set her free. After being rescued from the island and back at Cocoa Beach, Florida, Jeannie (played by Barbara Eden, [*right*] set about serving her master. However, her efforts to serve him resulted in confusing situations caused in part by her lack of familiarity with 20th-century American customs. Captain Roger Healey (played by Bill Daily) and Doctor Alfred Bellows (played by Hayden Rorke) rounded out the main cast.

Below: Larry Hagman, Barbara Eden and guest star Sammy Davis Jr. Several performers played themselves on *I Dream of Jeannie,* including Groucho Marx, Milton Berle, Don Ho, and Judy Carne and Arte Johnson from *Rowan & Martin's Laugh-In.*

Did you know?

The antique bottle that Jeannie called home was actually a decorative Jim Beam liquor decanter. The bottle was decorated and painted with gold leaf by the show's art department.

Right: Barbara Eden and Larry Hagman on the set of *I Dream Of Jeannie*.

Below: Married, at last!

237

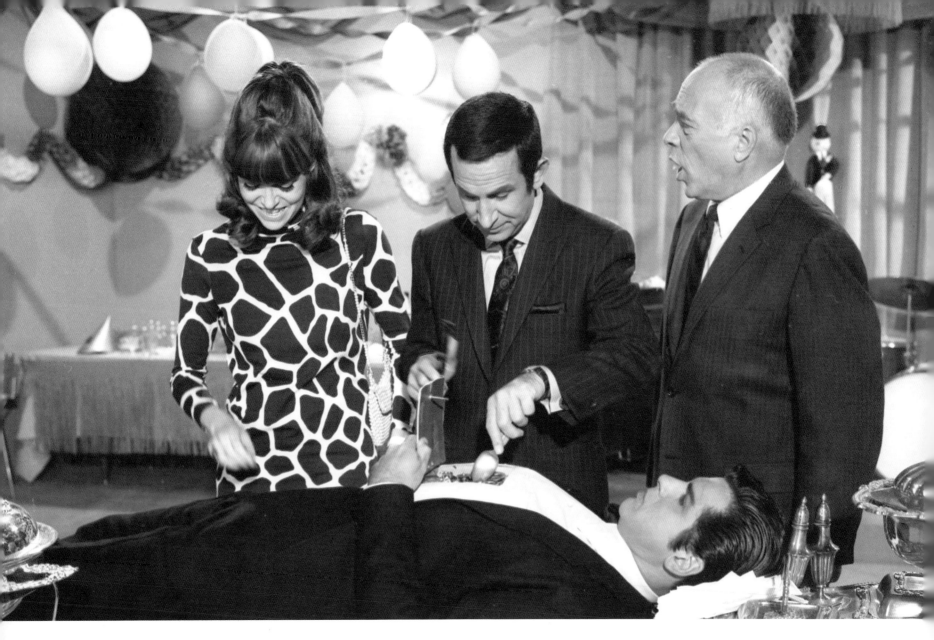

Get Smart

(18 September 1965–13 September 1969) **NBC**
(26 September 1969–11 September 1970) **CBS**

Created by Mel Brooks and Buck Henry, *Get Smart* parodied the espionage craze of the 1960s, with comedian Don Adams starring as CONTROL agent Maxwell Smart. Agent 99 was played by Barbara Feldon, while character actor Edward Platt (*Rebel Without a Cause*) was The Chief and Siegfried was Bernie Copell. Also featured from time to time in the battle against the laughably dark forces of KAOS were Robert Karvelas as Agent Larrabee and Dick Gautier as Hymie.

Above: Agent 99 and The Chief watch on as Max works on Hymie the Robot.

Did you know?

Agent 99's real name is never revealed, not even when she marries Smart, after which she was occasionally referred to as Mrs Smart. Bernie Kopell came to the show in the second season as Maxwell Smart's evil rival Siegfried. You might know Bernie better as Doctor Bricker on the show *Love Boat*.

Right: Don Adams stars as Maxwell Smart. Adams was a US Marine during World War II. He contracted malaria during the fighting in Guadalcanal. His TV career started when he won the competition on the TV show, *Ted Mack's Amateur Hour*.

Below: Don Adams and Fang on the cover of *TV Times* on 18 December 1968.

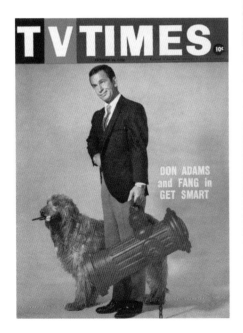

The Flying Nun

(7 September 1967–3 April 1970) **ABC**

Left: 'Some flying tips….It's very simple. If lift plus thrust is greater than load plus drag, you fly, and it doesn't matter whether you happen to be a nun or not'. Sister Bertrille (Sally Field) finds it rather difficult to explain to Sister Jacqueline (Marge Redmond), in an episode in July 1967.

Did you know?

In one episode, Sister Bertrille is looking at home movies of herself from when she was a teenager. The home movies were actually footage from Sally Field's previous series *Gidget* (1965). Patty Duke (*The Patty Duke Show*) was offered the role of Sister Bertrille but she turned it down. Then they offered the role to Sally Field (*Gidget*) and she turned it down, too. It was then offered to Ronnie Troup (*My Three Sons*), but Sally Field contacted them to say she had changed her mind.

Below: Sister Bertrille (Sally Field, *centre*) gets her first look at the Covent at San Tanco.

240

The Samurai
(7 October 1962–14 March 1965)

The adventures of Shintaro the Samurai, travelling 18th century Japan with his companion Tombei, battling the enemies of the Shogun and the dreaded Koga Ninjas was an enormous hit in Australia and other parts of the world.

Did you know?

The early 1960s cult favourite *The Samurai*, featuring Shintaro (Koichi Ose, left) and his companion Tombei the Mist (Fuyukichi Maki). Shintaro was such a favourite with Australian viewers that the show was said to even heal the animosity older Australians held for the Japanese after World War II. When Ose visited Australia in 1965, he was given a welcome that rivalled The Beatles the previous year.

Skippy, the Bush Kangaroo
(1 October 1968–3 March 1970)

Right: Veteran actor Ed Devereaux and youngster Garry Pankhurst with Skippy, the star of the series, on the cover of *TV Week* on 24 May 1969.

Hogan's Heroes
(17 September 1965–4 July 1971) **CBS**

Actor Bob Crane, who once had the number-one radio show in Los Angeles in the 1950s before branching out as an actor (*The Donna Reed Show* and *The Dick Van Dyke Show*) signed on for *Hogan's Heroes* (*left*), an unlikely comedy about a POW camp inspired by the 1953 film *Stalag 17*. Commandant of the camp was the incompetent Col. Klink (played by Werner Klemperer) and guarding Stalag 13, where the American-led resistance forces were housed, was the equally inept Sgt. Schultz (played by John Banner). Under the direction of Col. Robert Hogan (played by Bob Crane), the prisoners were actually in complete control of the camp. Other characters were Louis LeBeau (played by Robert Clary), Peter Newkirk (Richard Dawson), James Kinchloe (Ivan Dixon), Sgt. Richard Baker (Kenneth Washington), Sgt. Carter (Larry Hovis), Helga (Cynthia Lynn) and Hilda (Sigrid Valdis).

Opposite top: Bob Crane (*right*), John Banner (*centre*) and Werner Klemperer (*left*). Many critics questioned the decision to make a comedy about the Germans in World War II, but it never bothered the cast. Robert Clary, John Banner and Leon Askin were all survivors of the Holocaust, while Werner Klemperer had escaped Nazi Germany in 1933 before forging a career as a serious actor (*Judgment at Nuremberg*).

Bob Crane (*right*) was later sensationally murdered while on tour with a theatre company in 1978 and the lurid circumstances of his death were the basis of the 2002 film *Auto Focus*, starring Greg Kinnear.

Far right: Bob Crane and Sigrid Valdis, who would later become his second wife

The Sensational Seventies exploded onto our screens in a sea of "groovy" fashions, and stronger story-lines and more extreme situations and personalities. We were prepared to poke fun at ourselves, but we weren't afraid to tackle social issues previously deemed unsuitable for family viewing. Television was growing up, and it was showing a maturity and sophistication in both its production and story-lines. The comedy continued to flow, with shows such as *The Carol Burnett Show*, *All in the Family* and *Happy Days*; variety shows *The Sonny and Cher Comedy Hour* and *Donny and Marie* displayed the best talents of the era, while TV favourites Raymond Burr, Jack Lord and Mary Tyler Moore came back with new hits shows *Ironside*, *Hawaii Five-0* and *The Mary Tyler Moore Show* respectively. While there would always be Westerns on TV, the format evolved to showcase character development and social issues, such as in *Little House on the Prairie*. Detective shows flourished, with *Columbo* as the thinking-man's detective; *Kojak*, the hard nut; *The Streets of San Francisco*, a young gun alongside an old hand, and *The Mod Squad*, a hip trio of young cops. Johnny Carson continued his reign on late night TV but new stars, such as John Travolta in *Welcome Back Kotter*, were also being discovered. *The Brady Bunch* and *The Partridge Family* may have provided the ideal American family, but *MASH* broke new boundaries and became a television institution. Don't touch that dial!

Left: The cast of *The Brady Bunch* flank Sherwood Schwartz on the show's iconic staircase.

1970s

The Carol Burnett Show (Carol Burnett and Friends in syndication)

(11 September, 1967–29 March, 1978) **CBS**

Carol Burnett, a physical comedienne had earlier become familiar to the viewing public during her three seasons (1959–1962) on *The Garry Moore Show*. On her own show she brought together a group of talented players including: funny man Harvey Korman (replaced by Dick Van Dyke in 1977), the handsome Lyle Wagner (replaced by Tim Conway in 1975) and the talented newcomer Vicki Lawrence, who had a remarkable resemblance to Burnett. And while her support stars were all excellent it was Burnett herself who was superb as one of television's most individual, versatile performers, who could sing, dance, act, clown and mime with equal skill.

Left: Carol Burnett (*centre*), Harvey Korman, and Vicki Lawrence.

Below: *The Carol Burnett Show* on the cover of *TV Guide*.

Above: Vicki Lawrence, Carol Burnett, Mickey Rooney and John Davidson performing in 1968.

Right: Carol Burnett, Cher and Dennis Weaver on the show.

Did you know?

Each week's show was taped twice in front of different audiences and the best parts from each taping were edited together. Jim Nabors, star of *The Andy Griffith Show* (1960) and *Gomer Pyle, U.S.M.C.* (1964) was one of Ms. Burnett's dearest friends and appeared on the first episode of every single season. Carol Burnett considered him to be her 'good luck charm'.

Marcus Welby, M.D.
(23 September 1969–11 May 1976) **ABC**

Robert Young starred as Marcus Welby M.D., a veteran general practitioner whose thoroughness and dedication intersected the lives of a variety of patients who provided the central storyline of the series. Assisting him was Dr Steven Kiley played by James Brolin. The inevitable tension between youth and experience was established, but Welby often tended to be the more unorthodox of the two.

Below: Robert Young and James Brolin on the cover of *TV Week* on 27 June 1970.

Above: Dr Welby (Robert Young) tries to find a way to bring six-year-old Stewart (Brian Dewey), a boy with autism, out of his shell, as the youngster's mother (Lynn Carlin) looks on quietly in the episode 'The Foal'.

Right: Dr Welby tries to dissuade a depressed girl (Barbara Anderson) from taking her own life in the episode 'To Get Through The Night' in October 1970.

Did you know?

The exterior of Dr Welby's office was the same building used as the Cleaver family home on *Leave It to Beaver* (1957). Robert Young came out of a seven-year retirement to play the role of Welby at age 62.

Left: Salvatore 'Sonny' Bono and wife Cherilyn 'Cher' Sarkisan.

Below: Special guest star Truman Capote plays Admiral Nelson, with Sonny as his second in command, and Cher as Lady Hamilton in September 1973.

The Sonny and Cher Comedy Hour

(1 August 1971–29 May 1974) **CBS**

The Sonny and Cher Show

(1 February 1976–29 August 1977) **CBS**

After a few years of relative obscurity, 1960s pop sensations Sonny and Cher got their big break when their *Comedy Hour* debuted as a summer replacement, but quickly found its place in the midseason schedule. A freshness, combined with slick production, insured its chances of renewal. The combination of Sonny's enthusiasm and Cher's sardonic wit proved a winner with the viewers, as did the various musical numbers and special guests on the show. Utilising several recurring comedy sketches, such as 'The Vamp', performed by Cher, 'Sonny's Pizza' and 'Dirty Linen', regulars on the show included Peter Cullen, Freeman King, Teri Garr, Ted Zeigler, Billy Van and Murray Langston. While the pair looked the picture of happiness on air, they eventually divorced in 1974, bringing a premature end to the show. After each hosting unsuccessful variety shows, they reunited, but only on camera, in 1976 for a short-lived reprise of their show

Columbo

(15 September 1971–1 September 1978) **NBC**
(1989–2003)**ABC**

Peter Falk starred as Columbo, a cigar-smoking
police lieutenant who drove an old, beat-up car and
solved crimes with his unique, unorthodox approach.
Most shows followed the same formula: the crime
was committed at the beginning of the show when
the audience learned the identity of the culprit and
Columbo's beguilingly inept manor and dishevelled
appearance led the villain to underestimate him.
It was clear from the questions he asked, however, that
Columbo was nobody's fool and by the conclusion of
each episode he had unmasked the person responsible.

Right: Peter Falk won four Emmy
awards for his role as Columbo.

Below left: Peter Falk and Gene Barry star as the shrewd
police detective and a suave psychiatrist who fight a battle
of wits after the doctor's wife is found murdered in the
premier episode of *Columbo*, 'Prescription Murder'.

Below right: Don Ameche (*left*) appeared with
Columbo star Peter Falk in an episode
of the popular drama in 1971.

All in The Family
(later Archie Bunker's Place)

(12 January 1971–21 September 1983) CBS

All in the Family is arguably the single most influential programme in the history of broadcasting because of its impact on American audiences and on the style of television comedy. It was the first sitcom to be videotaped and performed before a live audience. The show's character and story development broke new ground in television. It was the first situation comedy to deal openly with social issues such as politics, bigotry, prejudice, birth control, abortion, menopause and homosexuality. Carroll O'Connor played Archie Bunker, a bigoted, right wing, lower-middle-class, white protestant, with a tendency to run his mouth. Jean Stapleton played Archie's devoted wife Edith Bunker. Patient, tolerant, even-tempered and honest, Edith was the heart of the show. Sally Struthers played Bunker's only child Gloria and Rob Reiner, son of Carl Reiner, her husband, Mike Stivic. His part was to continually bait the bigoted Archie into a confrontation.

Did you know?

All in the Family was modelled on the successful UK series *Til Death Do US Part.*

Opposite: *All in the Family.* (*Clockwise from top left*): Rob Reiner, Sally Struthers, Carroll O'Connor and Jean Stapleton.

Below opposite: Carroll O'Connor as Archie Bunker and Jean Stapleton as his wife Edith try to convince a government official (played by James O'Reare) that his computer erred when it reported Archie's death, in an October 1973 episode.

Right: Edith and Archie in a classic pose.

Below: Archie is indignant over a nurse's (Beatrice Colen) suggestion as to where he should receive a hypodermic injection in an episode which aired in October 1975.

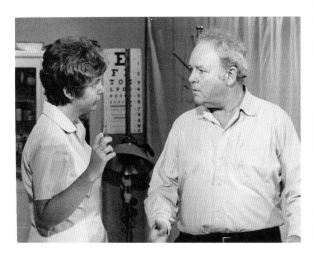

Did you know?

W. Mark Felt, the FBI associate director, later unmasked as the infamous Watergate informant *Deep Throat*, served as a technical advisor for the series. There was no lack of vintage cars to chase criminals and sometimes crash on *The FBI* TV show. The series' sponsor was the Ford Motor Company and they supplied all of the necessary Ford classics.

The FBI

(19 September 1965–8 September 1974) **ABC**

Produced with the cooperation of J. Edgar Hoover (the actual FBI Director), *The FBI* starred Efrem Zimbalist Jr. as Inspector Lewis Erskine, a calm man under pressure, with impeccable integrity but little humour. This long-running series portrayed the agency as a professional operation who tracked down their quarry methodically and scientifically. The cast included: Philip Abbott as Agent Arthur Ward, Stephen Brooks as agent Jim Rhodes, boyfriend of Erskine's daughter Barbara, Lynne Loring as Barbara Erskine, William Reynolds as Agent Tom Colby and Shelly Novack as Agent Chris Daniels.

Above: On filming location in the nation's capital, Efrem Zimbalist Jr. plays Inspector Lewis Erskine, star of *The FBI* at the start of the fourth season in 1968.

Right: Efrem Zimbalist Jr. and Joe Maross staging a fight on the set of *The FBI*.

The Tonight Show starring Johnny Carson
(1962–1992) **NBC**

Above: The peerless Johnny Carson interviews actor Peter Falk during the 1970s run of his top rating
The Tonight Show. Carson ruled the late-night airwaves on American television for three decades.

Till Death Us Do Part
(22 July 1965–16 December 1975)

Till Death Us Do Part was a British sitcom, which centred on the Garnett Family in the East End of London, with the head of the family, Alf Garnett (played by Warren Mitchell), a racist with anti-socialist views. Critics claimed Alf's views were not suitable for television and e aired many uncomfortable and disturbing opinions. The show also featured a key feature of British life in the 1960s, the widening generation gap. Some of Garnett's phrases in the series became his character's catchphrases, referring to his wife as 'You Silly Moo'.

Above: Una Stubbs and Warren Mitchell in *Till Death Us Do Part*.

Right: The *Till Death Us Do Part* cast on the cover of *TV Times*. Long-suffering wife Else (played by Dandy Nichols), daughter Rita (played by Una Stubbs) and Rita's intelligent but layabout husband Mike Rawlins (played by Anthony Booth).

Kojak
(24 October 1973–15 April 1978) **CBS**

Kojak (Telly Savalas) had a cynical sense of humour and was determined to do things his way regardless of what his bosses thought. Outspoken but streetwise, and not above stretching the law if it would help him crack a case, Kojak worked closely with plainclothes detective Bobby Crocker (Kevin Dobson) on location, mainly in New York.

Right: Telly Savalas as Kojak.

Did you know?
The lollipop was utilised by Telly Savalas to cut back on his smoking.

Alias Smith and Jones

(January 1971–January 1973) **ABC**

Loosely based on the adventures of *Butch Cassidy and the Sundance Kid*, *Alias Smith and Jones* proved to be a huge hit for their stars Ben Murphy and Peter Duel in the early 1970s. All that came to an end when Duel (who played the brother-in-law on the Sally Field series *Gidget*) took his own life on New Year's Eve, 1971, at the height of the show. His character was replaced by actor Roger Davies, but it was the end of the short-lived show and stardom for good-looking newcomer Ben Murphy.

Above: Guest star Burl Ives hires Ben Murphy to re-steal a stolen statue in the premier episode 'The McCreedy Bust'.

Right: Pete Duel (*left*) and Jack Cassidy on the set of *Alias Smith and Jones* in 1971.

Welcome Back Kotter

(September 9, 1975–June 8, 1979) ABC

Another smash hit based on an English comedy show (*Please Sir* 1969–73), *Welcome Back Kotter* owed more to the stand-up comedy of Gabe Kaplin, who played the title character of teacher Gabe Kotter. The movie success of breakout star John Travolta ultimately saw the show end—that and the fact that by 1979 the respective stars were in their mid to late 20s and had to graduate school sometime. Ron Palillo (Horhsak), Robert Hegyes (Juan Epstein) and Lawrence Hilton-Jacobs (Washington) rounded off the gang of 'Sweathogs' tamed by the wit and wisdom of Kaplan's character. The show also benefitted from killer theme song composed by 1960s star John Sebastian.

Did you know?

When the show ended, comic Gabe Kaplan later toured nationally in the role of Groucho Marx on stage. Robert Heyges often starred as Harpo.

Right: Ron Pallilo and Robert Hegyes (*back*), John Travolta, Gabe Kaplan and Lawrence Hilton-Jacobs (*front*). Pallilo and Hegyes both died of heart attacks with months of each other in 2012.

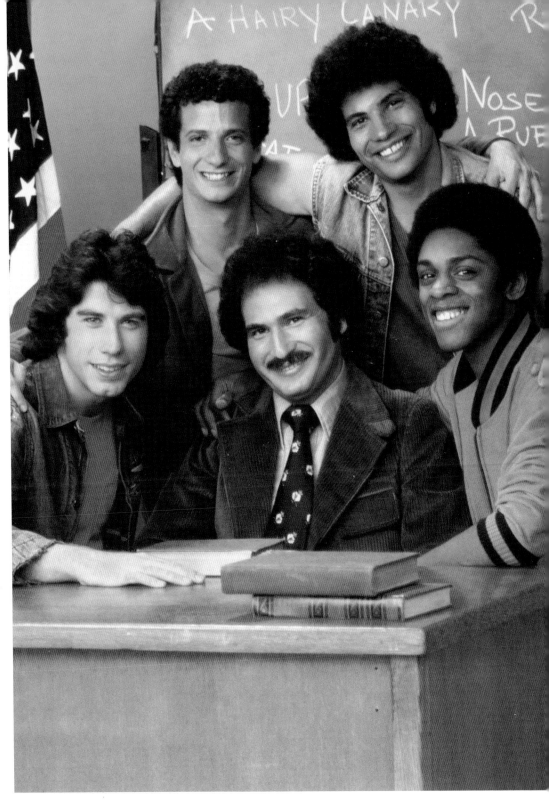

259

Did you know?

William Conrad narrated The Fugitive *Rocky, Bullwinkle, and Friends* (1961); *Buck Rogers in the 25th Century* (1979); *The Highwayman* (1988); and the 1977 mini-series: *How the West Was Won*. Much earlier, from 1952 to 1961, Conrad starred on the *Gunsmoke Radio Show* as Marshall Matt Dillon. He didn't take the role on the *Gunsmoke TV Show* because he felt that he was too fat for audiences to accept him as a tough guy. That didn't hurt him years later when he starred on *Cannon* (1971) and *Jake and the Fatman*.

Cannon

(14 September 1971–19 September 1976) **CBS**

Balding, middle-aged, and portly, detective Frank Cannon represented quite a change from the traditional suave, handsome private detectives TV viewers were used to. This crime show starred William Conrad as Frank Cannon, a former cop turned private eye. While television viewers might not have recognised Conrad's hefty frame, his voice was familiar: Conrad was radio's Matt Dillon on *Gunsmoke*, and narrated several television series including *Rocky and His Friends* and *The Fugitive*. *Cannon* was one of the few series during the 1970s with only one regular star.

Above: William Conrad as private investigator Frank Cannon is hired to protect Jessica Walter, who guests stars as an attorney whose life is threatened in the episode 'That Was No Lady'.

Right: Cannon to the rescue. William Conrad strives to absolve his friend's wife, played by Vera Miles, of a false murder charge in an episode of *Cannon* in March 1973.

260

The Mod Squad
(24 September 1968–23 August 1973) **ABC**

The Mod Squad series creator Buddy Ruskin, a former Los Angeles police officer, used his experiences with a special L.A.P.D. youth squad as the basis for this show. The series starred Peggy Lipton, Michael Cole and Clarence Williams III ('one black, one white and one blond')—as the voice-over informed us at the beginning of each show—as a 'hip' young team of undercover Los Angeles cops under the direction of veteran Captain Adam Greer, played by Tige Andrews (*The Detectives*). The executive producers of the show were Aaron Spelling and Danny Thomas.

Right: *The Mod Squad* cast with guest star Ida Lupino.

Below: *The Mod Squad* on the cover of *TV Week* on 22 August 1970.

Did you know?

Although the character, Stan Butler, was supposed to be in his mid-30s, Reg Varney was already 52 when the series began.

On the Buses

(28 February 1969–20 May 1973) UK

This popular English comedy starred Reg Varney as Stan Butler, a lowly bus driver, and his dysfunctional family and co-workers.

Left: *On The Buses* cast (*left to right*): Michael Robbins as Arthur Rudge (Stan's brother-in-law), Anna Karen as Olive Rudge, Reg Varney as Stan Butler, Doris Hare as Stan's mum, Bob Grant as Jack Harper (Stan's conductor), Stephen Lewis as 'Blakey' (Stan's inspector).

Below: *On the Buses* cast on the cover of *TV Week* on 17 June 1972.

The Benny Hill Show–UK
(20 August 1951–1 May 1989)

The pudgy comedian who always had a host of beautiful woman close by became something of a cult figure in his native Great Britain, and in 160 countries around the world. Benny Hill wrote much of his own material, was a fine musician and songwriter and an underrated physical comic and actor. Sexist, old-fashioned and smutty? Of course it was. But it was also bitingly funny at times, with Hill and troupe of talented comedians appearing in different formats of the show for almost four decades. The main supporting cast included Henry McGee, Bob Todd, Nicholas Parsons, Jon Jon O'Keefe and Jack Wright, with the regular females including Jenny Lee-Wright, Sue Bond, Cherri Gilham, Diana Darvey, Bettina Le Beau and Lesley Goldie.

Did you know?

Most of the material, both musical and scripted, was written by Benny Hill. He also frequently directed the show. While the show drew criticism for being sexist, Hill was quoted as saying, 'The female characters kept their dignity while the men were portrayed as buffoons'.

Right: Benny Hill with some of the ladies on the show.

Below: Benny Hill as Ernie (*He Drove the Fastest Milk Cart in the West*), which was a number-one hit song for him in the early 1970s.

Donny and Marie

(26 January 1976–12 May 1978)

Donny and Marie were the breakout stars of the extended Osmond family (*right*) who had performed on television since the early 1960s on The Andy Williams Show. Donny and Marie (*above*) produced a schmaltzy, family-orientated variety show but it was a lot of fun and very popular with audiences. It also pretty-much destroyed their respective careers before the pair found success again in the 2000s…first separately, and then together on stage in Las Vegas.

Barnaby Jones
(28 January 1973–3 April 1980) **CBS**

The venerable Buddy Ebsen (*right*),
fresh from his nine-season starring
role on *The Beverly Hillbillies*,
returned to our screens in this
popular detective series set in modern
day Los Angles. Ebsen played title
character Barnaby Jones alongside
actress Lee Meriwether as his
daughter-in-law for another seven
seasons in the 1970s.

The Brady Bunch
(26 September 1969–30 August 1974) **ABC**

A Sherwood Schwartz-created sitcom (also executive producer) about two one-parent families who come together to live as one, when a widower (Robert Reed who plays Mike Brady) with three sons marries a widow (Florence Henderson who plays Carol Brady) with three daughters. Throw in a nutty housekeeper (Alice played by Ann B. Davis), a cat and a shaggy dog and you fun a lot of fun. Other cast members included: Maureen McCormick as Marcia, Barry Williams as Greg, Eve Plumb as Jan, Christopher Knight as Peter, Susan Olsen as Cindy and Michael Lookinland as Bobby.

Opposite: The Brady Bunch, the All American family.

Above: Carol and Mike Brady with the three girls, Marcia, Jan and Cindy.

The New Bill Cosby Show
(11 September 1972–7 May 1973) **CBS**

This was an hour-long variety show hosted by and starring comedian Bill Cosby, which showcased both the guest stars as well as the regulars. Some of the regulars included: Lola Falana, Foster Brooks, Oscar deGruy and Susan Tolsky, while Quincy Jones conducted the orchestra. The Donald McKayle Dancers also featured. Two of the regular sketches were 'The Wife of the Week' and 'The Dude', a character who was just too cool.

Left: *The New Bill Cosby Show* in 1972.

Below top: Oscar-winner Sidney Poitier (*right*) and Emmy Award-winner Harry Belafonte (*left*) flank Bill Cosby as guests on the premier show, 1972.

Below bottom: Guest star Ray Charles joins host Bill Cosby in the song *Look What They've Done to My Song Ma*.

Are You Being Served?

(8 September 1972–1 April 1985) UK

Brilliantly cast, the series follows the madcap misadventures and mishaps of workers in a fictional London department store, Grace Brothers. Set amongst the ladies' and gentleman's clothing area *Are You Being Served* featured humour based largely on sexual innuendo, various misunderstandings and the odd awkward moment. At the forefront of the comedy, however, was a merciless parody of the British class system, with characters rarely addressing themselves by their first name, rather 'Mr', 'Mrs', or even 'Captain'.

The main cast members included Mrs Betty Slocombe, head of the ladies department, Mr Wilberforce Claybourne Humphries, a gay man who lives with his mother, Captain Stephen Peacock, the haughty floorwalker, Miss Shirley Brahms, an attractive working-class junior, Mr Ernest Grainger, a 40-year veteran who often fell asleep while at work, Mr Cuthbert Rumbold, the bumbling and incompetent floor manager, Mr James 'Dick' Lucas, the young womaniser and Young Mr Grace, the very old and rich, but also stingy, store owner, who usually appeared surrounded by young and attractive women.

Left: *Emergency* stars Randolph Mantooth (*left*) and Kevin Tighe in 1972.

Below: Robert Fuller in *Emergency* in 1972.

Emergency

(22 January 1972–3 September 1977) **NBC**

Emergency was a fast-moving show which depicted the efforts of a team of paramedics assigned to Squad 51 of the Los Angeles County Fire Department and associated with nearby Ramparts General Hospital. Stars of the show were Kevin Tighe as Paramedic Roy DeSoto and Randolph Mantooth as Paramedic John Gage. Each telecast depicted several interwoven incidents, some humorous, some touching, while some were tragic.

Did you know?

The series is popularly credited for encouraging the widespread adoption of paramedic programs across North America.

The Morecombe and Wise Show
(1968–1977) UK

Right: Eric Morecombe and Ernie Wise were a British comic team that worked from 1941 until Morecombe's death in 1984, in a variety of radio, film and most successfully television.

The Two Ronnies
(10 April 1971–25 December 1987)

Given their own show by the BBC in 1971, Ronnie Barker and Ronnie Corbett quickly became one of the most successful and long-running light entertainment shows on British television, attracting 20 million viewers a show at its peak. The brilliantly complementary personalities of the two worked perfectly as they featured in comic sketches both together and separately. Over the years the show had some notable writers, including John Cleese and Spike Milligan, while Ronnie Barker used the pseudonym Gerald Wiley when writing sketches. Some of the sketches would often involve complex word-play, much of it written by Barker. Corbett would appear quieter, more often acting as a foil for Barker, with the chemistry working perfectly.

Ironside
(14 September 1967–16 January 1975 **NBC**

After playing Perry Mason, Raymond Burr had another hit on his hands playing paraplegic Chief of Detectives, Robert T. Ironside.

Below top: Chief Ironside (Raymond Burr) scrutinizes a Zeppelin stamp, a clue to the murder of an English police official, as Det. Sgt. Ed Brown (Don Galloway), English Police Supt. Faber (Lloyd Bochner) and stamp dealer Muller (Stefan Gierasch) look on, in 'Shadow Soldier', aired in November 1972.

Below bottom: Raymond Burr as Detective Robert T. Ironside and Don Mitchell as the delinquent-turned-bodyguard/assistant Mark Sanger, who opted to become a police officer, and subsequently graduated from law school.

Hawaii Five-0

(26 September 1968–26 April 1980) **CBS**

This was television's longest-running crime show, filmed entirely on location in Hawaii. The show starred Jack Lord as Steve McGarrett, a no-nonsense head of Five-0, a special investigative unit directly responsible to the governor of Hawaii. Included in McGarrett's team were: James MacArthur as 'Danno' Williams, McGarrett's number-one assistant, Kam Fong as Chin Ho Kelly and Zulu as Kono. Jack Lord was also actively involved in many aspects of the show's production.

Above: Jack Lord, James MacArthur and Kam Fong in 'Honor is an Unmarked Grave', directed by Jack Lord.

Above: Jack Lord, Susan Kay Logan and Karol Kai.

Did you know?

Despite the attention that *Hawaii Five-0* brought to Hawaii's law enforcement, Hawaii is the only American state that has no state police agency. Jack Lord was the only cast member who stayed on *Hawaii Five-0* throughout its full twelve-year run.

The Partridge Family
(25 September 1970–31 August 1974) ABC

The Partridge Family (above) was based on the success of *The Cowsills*, a singing family that had great success in the late 1960s. Producers opted for a better looking 'TV' family who could act! Oscar-winner Shirley Jones (*Emer Gantry*, 1960) was the widowed mother of the musical troupe, and the show propelled David Cassidy (as Keith Partridge) to global superstardom in the 1970s.

Above: Danny Bonaduce as Danny and Susan Dey as Laurie, in *The Partridge Family*.

Did you know?

Shirley Jones was David Cassidy's step-mother in real life, having married David's father, character actor Jack Cassidy, in the late 1950s. Jones and Cassidy were the only actors to sing on the show...the other kids just mimed.

The Streets of San Francisco

(16 September 1972–23 June 1977) ABC

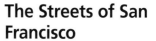

Filmed entirely on location in San Francisco, this hour-long crime show starred Karl Malden as Detective Lt. Mike Stone, a streetwise veteran, with Michael Douglas as his young partner, Inspector Steve Keller, while Lee Harris played Lt. Lessing. Against the backdrop of the Bay Area, these two detectives used modern police methods to track down criminals. By 1976, Mike Douglas left the show and was replaced by Inspector Dan Robbins, played by Richard Hatch.

Left: Karl Malden and Michael Douglas in the episode 'The Thrill Killers'.

Left: Michael Douglas and Karl Malden.

Right: Karl Malden starred as veteran detective Lt. Mike Stone.

Did you know?

While he acted on the show, Michael Douglas produced the Oscar-winning movie *One Flew Over the Cuckoo's Nest* (1975) for close friend Jack Nicholson. Douglas later won the Best Actor Oscar for 1987's *Wall Street*.

The Waltons
(14 September 1972–20 August 1981) **CBS**

The Waltons told the story of a close-knit family living in rural Virginia, with the story starting in the Depression years. The genesis was a Christmas special, 'The Homecoming', written by its creator Earl Hammer Jr., which was based on his own experiences (the same material had been given the 'Hollywood' treatment in the film *Spencer's Mountain* in 1964, starring Henry Fonda). After attracting such a favourable response, CBS decided to build a series around the Walton family that Hammer had created. The cast included: Richard Thomas as John Boy (1972–77, then Robert Wightman 1979–81); Ralph White as John Walton, Michael Learned as his wife Olivia Walton, Will Geer as Zeb (Grandpa) Walton, Ellen Corby as Esther (Grandma) Walton, Judy Norton-Taylor as Mary Ellen, David W. Harper as Jim-Bob, Kami Cotler as Elizabeth, Jon Walmsley as Jason, Mary Elizabeth McDonough as Erin and Eric Scott as Ben Walton. The series was told through the eyes of John Boy, the eldest son, who wanted to be a novelist.

Above: Flanking host Carl Reiner (*centre*) are Mel Brooks, Peggy Cass, Ron Carey, Don Adams and Tony Randall. Many established comedians from the 1950s and 1960s continued to have an influence into the new decade, while some established stars such as Jerry Colonna (*pictured right*) found it difficult to relate to a younger audience.

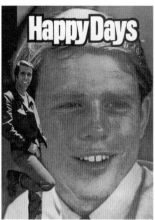

Happy Days
(15 January 1974–August 1984) **ABC**

Happy Days was created by Garry Marshall, an experienced comedy writer who had worked on hits like *The Dick Van Dyke Show* and *The Lucy Show*, as well as producing *The Odd Couple*. After a slow start, *Happy Days* finally cracked Nielsen's top ten in its third season, before reaching number one a year later. A sitcom set in 1950s Milwaukee, and based around the Cunningham family, Ron Howard (*The Andy Griffith Show*) was Richie, Tom Bosley was his father Howard, Marion Ross was his mother Marion, Erin Moran his younger sister Joanie. Richie had three close friends: Anson Williams was Warren 'Potsie' Webber, Donny Most was Ralph Malph and Henry Winkler was Arthur 'Fonzie' Fonzarelli. Fonzie proved to be the breakout character on the show. By season three, Fonzie was the focal point of the series.

Above: Henry Winkler as Fonzie, Donny Most as Ralph Malph, Anson Williams as Potsie and Ron Howard as Richie Cunningham in the 1975 episode 'Fonzie Moves in'.

Above right: Tom Bosley (*right*) as Howard Cunningham, breaks the news to wife Marion (Marion Ross) that their son Richie (Ron Howard) has arranged for pal, Potsie, to impersonate him on a blind date with the daughter of one of Mr Cunningham's clients.

Right: Ron Howard and Henry Winkler in the early days of *Happy Days*. Note Fonzie's jacket.

Did you know?

Censors would not allow Fonzie to wear a leather jacket in the earliest episodes, fearing it would promote a delinquent stereotype, but gradually relaxed that stance as Henry Winkler's popularity grew. Many fans agree that the show's quality deteriorated after the three-part season 5 opener, 'Hollywood', where Fonzie jumps a shark while water-skiing. Today, when a show takes a sharp drop in quality, it's said to "jump the shark."

Right: Ralph Malph (Donny Most, *right*) is impressed with Richie's (Ron Howard's) family venture to build a bomb shelter in the episode, 'Be the First on Your Block', which aired in May 1974.

Little House on the Prairie
(11 September 1974–20 September 1982) **NBC**

While Michael Landon was the star of the show as Charles Ingalls, a struggling farmer trying to make a living for his young family, he was also executive producer as well as frequent writer and director. His initial family members included: Karen Grassle as the mother, Caroline Ingalls; Melissa Sue Anderson as their eldest daughter, Mary; Melissa Gilbert as their second daughter, Laura; twins Lindsay and Sidney Greenbush as the third daughter, Carrie; while a fourth daughter was born in the third season and was played by twins Wendi and Brenda Turnbeaugh. The stories were told through the point of view of their second daughter Laura. Although the time was set in the late 1870s and the location was the American west, this was not your traditional Western, but rather the trials and tribulations of a loving family during difficult times.

Above: The family is all decked out in finery, but it's only in a dream Laura has when she thinks she has found gold in 1975 episode, At the End of the Rainbow. From left to right are the father, the mother, Mary, Laura and Carrie.

Right: Karen Grassle (*left*), Michael Landon and Patricia Neal.

Right: 'The Wedding'. Linwood Boomer, Melissa Sue Anderson and Michael Landon. When executive producer and chief writer Landon ran out of material, he made the decision to deviate from source material the show was based on *The Little House on the Prairie* books by Laura Ingalls Wilder. In this particular story arch, TV daughter Melissa Sue Anderson goes blind, marries and later perishes in a house fire.

Below: Laura Ingalls (Melissa Gilbert) is heartbroken when she has to say goodbye to her father, Charles Ingalls (Michael Landon) at the end of the series.

MASH

(17 September 1972–28 February 1983) **CBS**

MASH refers to the 4077th Mobile Army
Surgical Hospital, stationed close to the
action during the Korean War. Their
job was to treat the wounded evacuated
from the front lines and to try and save
as many lives as possible. Based on the
1970 movie, *MASH* was much more
comedic and less ironic than Altman's
anti-war masterpiece. Two of the surgeons
were Hawkeye Pierce played by Alan
Alda (*left*) and Trapper John McIntyre
played by Wayne Rogers (*right*). Other
characters featured were Frank Burns
(Larry Linville), Hot Lipps Houlihan
(Loretta Swit), the commanding officer
Henry Blake (McLean Stevenson),
Radar O'Reilly, played by Gary Burghoff,
the only crossover from the original
movie, and cross-dressing Cpl. Maxwell
Klinger played by Jamie Farr.

Above: Alan Alda, Mike Farrell and Harry Morgan. Farrell replaced Wayne Rogers for the 1975–76 season and Morgan replaced McLean Stevenson the same year.

Right: Actress Loretta Swit (*right*) on the set of MASH with fellow cast members William Christopher (left) and Harry Morgan (*centre*).

The Mary Tyler Moore Show
(19 September 1970–3 September 1977) **CBS**

The Mary Tyler Moore Show was one of the enduring comedies of the 1970s. Mary Tyler Moore played Mary Richards, a single woman who settled in Minneapolis in an apartment after calling it quits with her boyfriend. Mary landed a job as associate producer of the evening news at WJM-TV, Channel 12, the city's lowest-rating station. The premise of the show was Mary, who was the calm, level-headed professional, usually at the centre of a storm of work arguments of a group of zany characters, which included: Edward Asner as the gruff boss Lou Grant, Gavin MacLeod as Murray Slaughter, the quick-witted news writer, Ted Knight, the dense and self-centered anchorman, while Valerie Harper played Rhoda Morgenstern, Mary's upstairs neighbour. Cloris Leachman was Phyllis Lindstrom, Mary's high-strung landlady and Georgie Engel was Georgette Franklin, Ted Baxter's naïve girlfriend.

Above: Georgette turns a quiet dinner party into pandemonium when she announces she is about to give birth. Lou Grant on left, Ted Knight and Mary.

Above: Mary goes over the finer points of the script with co-star Georgie Engel for the episode marking her debut.

Above: Gavin McLeod, Ted Knight and Mary Tyler Moore.

Left: The always lovely Mary Tyler Moore as the independent,
liberated professional 'Mary Richards' in her 1970 hit TV Show.

Did you know?

In reality the kitten in the MTM logo is yawning. Since the cameraman couldn't get a usable shot of the cat
actually meowing, the footage was used and a meow dubbed in

Dedication

I dedicate this book to my beloved and much missed mother Agnes.
Together we spent countless happy times watching many of the television shows in this book.

Ian Collis is a leading authority on sporting history and statistics and is the Head of Fox Sports Statistics, which delivers statistics solutions across all the major sporting codes. Ian also has one of the largest and most diverse collections of memorabilia and associated ephemera, covering sport, and the history of television. He is also the author of 22 books, including: *Retro Sydney, The Way We Used to Live* (2013), *St George: Eleven Golden Years of the Dragons* (2013), *Cricket Through the Decades* (2012), *Rugby League Through the Decades* (2011).

This edition published in 2014 by New Holland Publishers Pty Ltd
London • Sydney • Auckland

The Chandlery Unit 114 50 Westminster Bridge Road London SE1 7QY United Kingdom
1/66 Gibbes Street Chatswood NSW 2067 Australia
218 Lake Road Northcote Auckland New Zealand

www.newhollandpublishers.com

Copyright © 2014 New Holland Publishers Pty Ltd
Copyright © 2014 in text: Ian Collis
Copyright © 2014 in images: Ian Collis and NHP

All rights reserved. No part of this publication may be reproduced, stored in a retrieval system or transmitted, in any form or by any means, electronic, mechanical, photocopying, recording or otherwise, without the prior written permission of the publishers and copyright holders.

Every endeavour was made to source the original copyright holders of images in this book.

A record of this book is held at the British Library and the National Library of Australia.

ISBN 9781742575599

Managing Director: Fiona Schultz
Publisher: Alan Whiticker
Project Editor: Emily Carryer
Designer: Peter Guo
Production Director: Olga Dementiev
Printer: Toppan Leefung Printing Ltd (China)

10 9 8 7 6 5 4 3 2 1

Keep up with New Holland Publishers on Facebook
www.facebook.com/NewHollandPublishers

US $29.99
UK £19.99